MOB VI

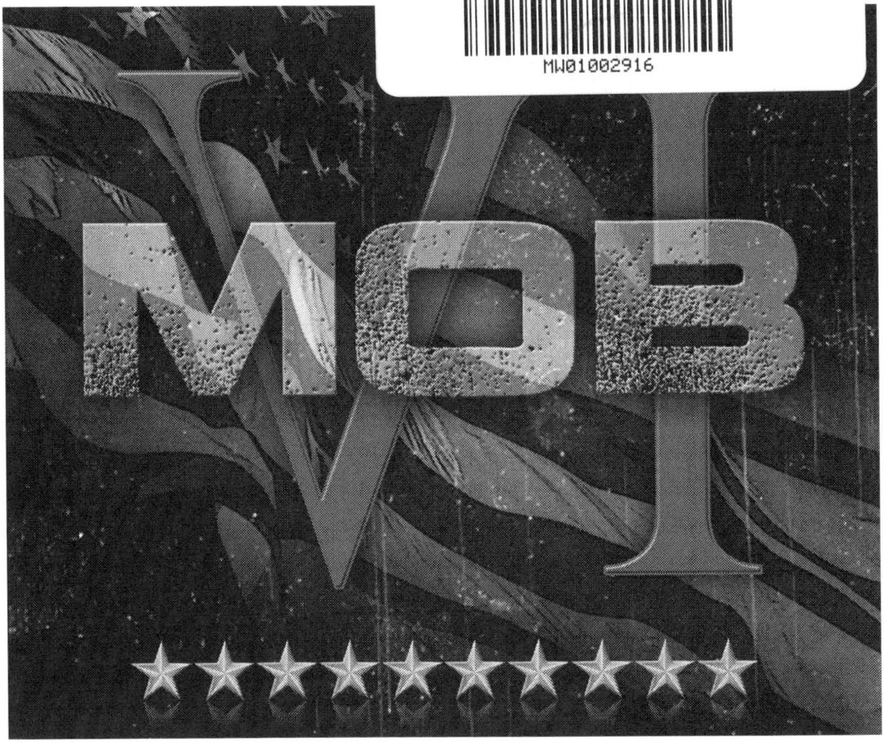

BY
JUSTIN K. SHEFFIELD

ILLUSTRATED BY: JOEY NOBODY

MOB VI is based on the life of Justin Sheffield while he was in the Navy. Other than the Gospel of the Lord Jesus Christ, people, places, names, and events have been fictionalized.

MOB VI

First Edition: 2020

Printed in the United States of America

10 9 8 7 6 5 4 3 2 1

This book is a work of fiction. Names, characters, places and incidents are either products of the author's imagination or are used fictitiously. Any resemblance to actual persons, living or dead, or locales is entirely coincidental.

ISBN-13: 978-0-9987704-1-3 (Paperback)
ISBN-13: 978-1-948035-58-3 (ebook)

Edited by Janet Musick
Cover designed by Spomenka Bojanic
Interior designed by Debbi Stocco

Published by Defiance Press and Publishing, LLC

Bulk orders of this book may be obtained by contacting Defiance Press and Publishing, LLC. www.defiancepress.com.

Public Relations Dept. – Defiance Press & Publishing, LLC
281-581-9300
pr@defiancepress.com

Defiance Press & Publishing, LLC
281-581-9300
info@defiancepress.com

TABLE OF CONTENTS

Chapter 1
NIGHTMARE

On a pitch black night in 2006, somewhere near the border of Afghanistan and Pakistan high in the Himalayas, I found myself reciting Psalm 91 under my breath as I climbed.

> *"He that dwelleth in the secret place of the most High shall abide under the shadow of the Almighty. I will say of the Lord, He is my refuge and my fortress, my God, in Him will I trust."*

I could hear the crisp sound of gravel crunching under my shoes as I walked over and sat down to catch my breath. I had just climbed three thousand feet, and my troop was strung out down the mountain, still climbing. I looked over at Johnny, who already had his shoe off and was banging a rock out.

"I've had that damned rock in my shoe for the last two hours, bro," he griped.

We were both drenched in sweat, high up on bald terrain. The stars were like an explosion in the sky. It's hard to describe the vast expanse of those mountains. I looked down and saw the rest of the guys appearing about fifty meters below.

"See anything?" I glanced at Johnny over my shoulder as I continued to count heads. Johnny just shook his head.

"I'm already out of water," I mumbled as I tried my Camelbak. My lips were starting to crack and my mouth was completely dry.

Johnny nodded, "That shit was gone a long time ago."

I threw a dip of Copenhagen in.

Over comms, I heard Sonny, the troop chief, pass the update: "2-Troop, this is 2-2. We're gonna take a quick five, let guys get some water."

Shane was coming up the trail as I replaced the dip can in my pocket. I watched him hesitate for a moment, then turn and raise his gun.

"Whoa, whoa, whoa," he said nervously.

'Whoa, whoa, whoa' isn't right. It wasn't a normal sound coming from Shane. I looked over and saw four dudes standing not thirty meters from us. One guy had an RPG and he was already pointing it straight down at our position. He'd clearly heard us, but it was too late. I leveled my laser on his chest and started dumping rounds. That guy just crumbled like a sack of shit in a little heap. I swung my barrel over to the next guy. Without a word among us, we opened up into their line. It happened so fast. Another enemy fighter dropped, and then another, as more fighters emerged from the rock outcroppings and began returning fire from their belt-fed PKMs and AK-47s.

Johnny was ahead of me, about ten yards up the ridge. We were both hunkered down behind these small boulders, trying to get as small as possible. It seemed like tracer fire was coming in from every direction. We could feel small rocks hitting us from the ricochets and then I heard Johnny muffled and yelling down at me, "I think I'm hit, bro."

I got up on a knee and dumped another two rounds into this Muslim's face, and his head came apart like a piñata. I did a quick mag change and told Johnny, "Come on back, bro. Just stay low. I got you covered."

Johnny worked his way to me and immediately pulled his shirt up. "Bro, check me, man, I think I'm hit. I felt something hit me."

I looked at his side through my NVGs and could see blood but no punctures. "Calm down, bro, you're good. Holy shit, bro, there's more there!"

I shouted and pointed as we dove to more cover behind rocks.

"Contact!"

There were four more bad guys blazing down at us. I looked over at Shane and a couple of the other guys that had made it up. They began flanking the enemy shooting at us from the high ground. Shane goes gangster-style with his MP7 on full automatic. Other guys were starting to make their way up now and picked up the fight.

"Dude, we're in a really bad spot," Shane yelled at me.

"No shit," I shouted. "Did you see where those other four fighters went?"

I could hear 2-2 come over the comms. "Troops in contact, troops in contact. Recce's in contact. Get your asses up there now."

Due to the steep terrain, our patrol had been spread out quite a ways and the guys that were still climbing hadn't quite made it up yet, but could hear the fireworks going on at the top of the mountain.

When I looked down off the ridge to my nine o' clock, Sonny and Noah were moving hastily below and getting a bite on the enemy. They set up an L ambush on 'em and one of the fighters opened up with an AK-47. Noah face-shot that guy and I heard "RPG!" as a rocket-propelled grenade went screaming past the right side of my head.

"Holy shit," I roared, "that was close!"

I spun around my Recce M4 and married my laser up with RPG boy's frantic face and squeezed two in rapid succession. That sent this asshole's head into pieces, and his body literally flipped off the side of a four thousand-foot cliff. It was movie-worthy. Between the eruptions of gunfire, I could hear guys gurgling and moaning, going through their death rattles.

Then I heard something very different. I heard a child screaming. And my heart sank as I realized that I recognized the voice of that little child.

"Daddy, Daddy, please!"

It's my son! My mind raced. How was he there? How had he gotten into this? I screamed back into the darkness as I ditched my kit and sprinted up the hill toward the tiny voice. "Daddy's coming. Please, Jesus, Daddy's coming, Bubba. Just hold on."

But, as I rounded a boulder where I thought he must be, I felt a hot sting as bullets entered my chest. I slumped to my knees and fell to the ground, the wind knocked out of me. I could taste the blood welling up in my mouth as I tried to mutter, "I'm sorry, Bubba, Daddy's so sorry…"

I could feel my arms and legs beginning to go numb as I struggled to stay conscious. I could just make out the shadowy figure of an enemy fighter coming into view in the darkness. I could hear him speaking in Pashtu as he leveled his AK at me and…

"Justin! Justin! Justin, wake up, please!" my wife pleaded with me from the foot of my bed. I started to come to and realized I was completely covered in sweat and had apparently been yelling out in my sleep. It was 7:35 in the morning and I was still trying to grasp the reality that I was not shot and my son was downstairs safely playing with his LEGOs.

"I'm sorry. Was I bad?" was all I could manage to say to her.

"Baby, you have to talk to someone. Please. I don't know what to do anymore."

"I know. I will. I will." I knew it was getting bad.

"Do you want to go with us to take Landon to school?" she asked.

"You guys go ahead. I'm all right. Just need to clear my head," I said.

"Okay," she said. "Are you sure you're okay?"

"I'm good. Promise. Love you."

My wife left the room and I listened until I heard the front door close and the unmistakable sound of the key turning the deadbolt. I sat up in bed and opened the drawer of the night stand. I pulled out a worn Bible and a small revolver and walked over to the closet. I reached up and pulled the cord on a single bulb hanging in the center and sat down Indian-style on the floor. I laid the Bible, the revolver, and a handful of rounds on the carpet and stared at them for a minute.

I looked at the Bible while I picked up the empty revolver and placed it next to my ear, listening as I pulled the trigger to the crisp sound of metal striking metal as the hammer fell on each empty cylinder. At this point, I could feel the tears running down my face. This was it, I thought. I placed a single round into a chamber of the revolver and raised the gun to my temple.

"Daddy? Daddy? Are you in there? Why are you crying?"

I guess my wife had forgotten something and had come back in for it. I never heard the bolt turn or the door open. My son had made his way upstairs looking for me. I quickly hid the gun under my leg as he opened the door. I wiped my face. "I'm okay, Bubba. Where's Mommy? I thought y'all left."

My wife walked into the bedroom and quickly put together what was happening. She scooped up my son and started to speak, her voice shaking.

"Baby, no! We have to get help. If not for you, do it for us. Do it for him."

I remember thinking to myself, "How did I ever get *here*? This would never be *my* story."

I'd love to tell you that, as a Christian, I was praying for Jesus to show up in a big way and save me from myself. But, if I'm honest after everything I'd been through, I was just praying for Christ to give me an excuse to end it all. I wanted to be done.

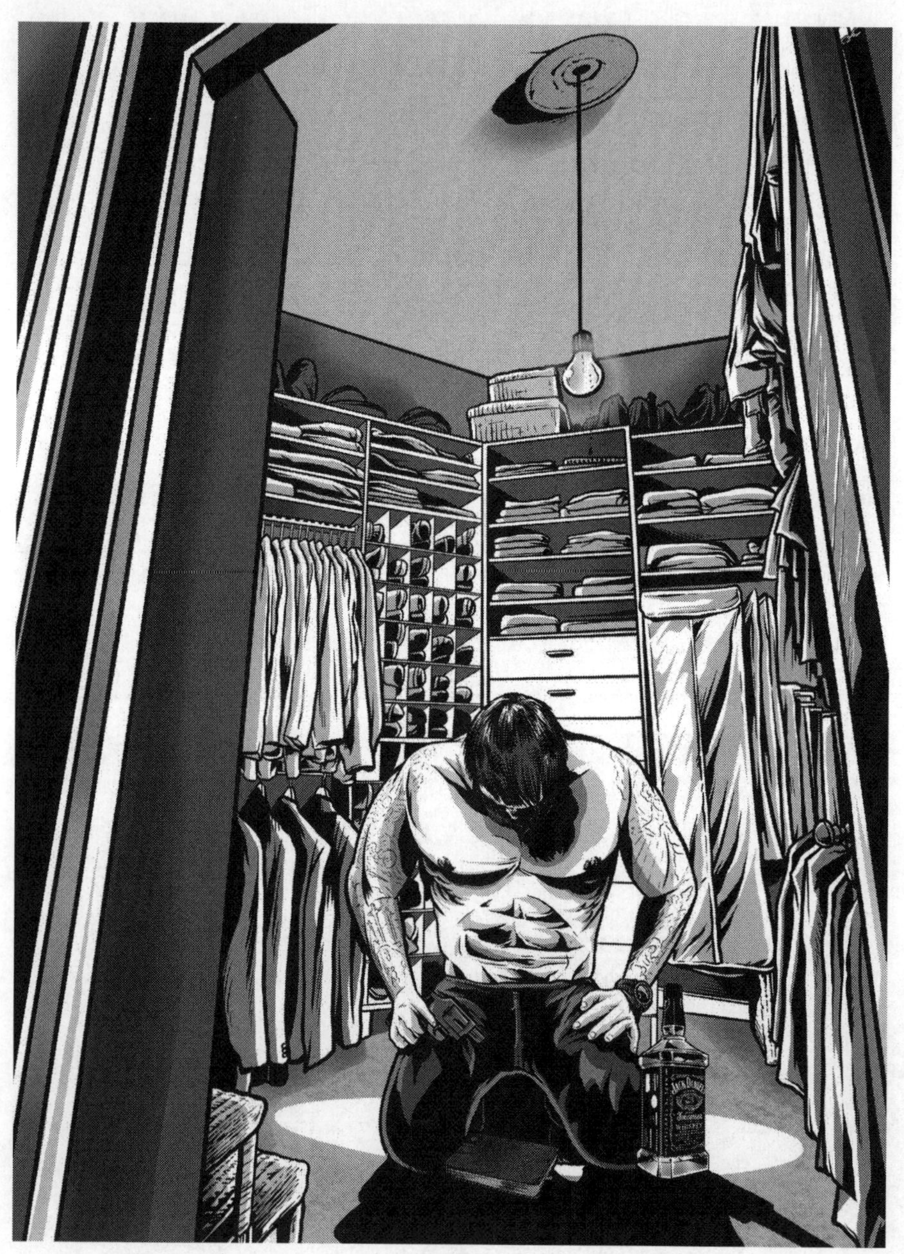

Chapter 2
IN THE BEGINNING

"WHAT'S YOUR NAME, FUCK FACE?"

As soon as I opened my mouth to answer, he yelled "Everyone hit the surf!"

The BUD/S instructors took us outside and ran us to the shore and, for the next two hours, we ran and swam in the freezing water and paused only for push-ups, sit-ups and flutter kicks until I could feel the muscles in my stomach getting ready to burst. The only break we got was to briefly cover ourselves in sand until we looked like sugar cookies.

That was my morning, day one, week one, and we hadn't even had breakfast yet…

Here's the deal. BUD/S is like the movie G.I. Jane except there is no way a chick could ever get through one day, let alone one week.

In August of 2000, six months after I enlisted, I got my shot at BUD/S, along with one-hundred-fifty other guys. I flew to San Diego, arriving at the Naval Special Warfare Training Center in Coronado at two o'clock in the morning, and there was no one there to welcome me or tell me what the hell to do. I didn't mind. I found an empty bunk and three hours later I was awakened by a commotion.

Turned out that most of the guys had checked in days or weeks prior to me getting there, and the bulk of the class had already formed. They had shiny boots, with their names already hand-stenciled across the back of the ankle. They were wearing starched camouflage uniforms with white t-shirts and spotless pants, pressed to the point they could stand up on their own. They were wide-awake, clean-shaven, and ready to seize the day, while I was half-asleep and in a daze and couldn't find my own asshole or a place to use it. The first day of BUD/S was much like the first time I pulled the trigger on another human being; it's something I'd never forget.

When I was about sixteen, my dad gave me the book Rogue Warrior. I was from West Texas, nowhere near the ocean, but I knew then that the SEAL Teams were something I wanted to be a part of. Then, that same year, my mom took me to an air show and I watched Navy SEAL Leap Frogs sky dive. I'd wanted to be a Navy SEAL ever since.

I moved to Austin after high school, and moved in with my brother. He was going to UT at the time. I started taking courses at the community college, but I still couldn't shake the desire I had for the SEAL Teams.

I didn't last a year in college. One night, driving home to San Angelo with a buddy, I got stopped for speeding. I was underage with an empty beer keg in the back of my truck and that's all the cause those two fat shit cops needed to search my truck. Long story short, I ended up with a felony charge for possession of a controlled substance and a misdemeanor for the absolute abundance of weed I had. Those two dicks took my keg, too.

Sitting there in jail gave me some time to reflect. It was the second time I'd been arrested in a year. I could say it wasn't my fault, but that's bullshit. It was my fault. I felt like a piece of shit. I remember seeing my mom and brother through the cell bars and then I saw my dad come in. I didn't want to face him. But he's my dad. I told them I was sorry and that I messed up. My folks were disappointed but mostly just happy I was okay. Then me and my brother shared a pack of smokes in his car as he drove me separately back to San Angelo.

After being on house arrest for a year and going to college back home, I started dating Leslie. I didn't know it right away, but she would later become my wife. I couldn't leave the house except for work, school, or church. I used to go to this college church group on Wednesday night because it's how I could get out of the house. I met Leslie there. We ended up spending all our time together.

I eventually told her I was over college and wanted to enlist in the Navy and be a Navy SEAL. I had been training my ass off. Working out, running five miles of hills and swimming was my daily routine. Leslie was very supportive. She knew I was going in no matter what. It still took an Act of God to get the district attorney to reverse and drop all charges. It took lots of prayer and letters from every coach, teacher, and preacher I knew in town to convince the DA I wasn't a screw-up. With those charges in place, guilty as I was, no branch of service would take me.

The guy was an ex-Ranger, thank God. He looked at me and said, "Son, you want to be a Navy SEAL?"

I said, "Yes, sir, with all my heart; it's the only thing I want to do. I'm sorry for what I did and I will not let anyone down." Some shit like that.

The DA said, "Young man, someone gave me a second chance once, and I'm gonna do the same for you. I expect that you'll remember this bit of mercy we showed you and maybe someday you'll have the same kind of opportunity with someone else."

I couldn't believe it. The charges were dropped. I went to the Navy recruiting station and enlisted that week. I still remember going to the mall in my hometown at 5:00 a.m. and getting on a bus that would take me to San Antonio, Texas. This was where the regional MEPS (Military Entrance Processing Station) was for my part of Texas.

Man, what a culture shock. They started right there stripping away my civil identity and making me into a service member. It was straight to a host of doctors for a physical, into a classroom for a litany of paperwork and a test. It was called the ASVAB (Armed Services Vocational Aptitude Battery) and basically was like the SAT for the military. Along with my physical, it helped them identify what jobs I could qualify for.

Then they took us into a little dark room with one light on and an American flag covering the wall. I had to stand there at attention with all the others that were joining the military that day. We all raised our right hands. I had chills, man; it was awesome.

A soldier in uniform came in and started, "Raise your right hands. Repeat after me!"

I repeated the oath. "I, Justin Sheffield, do solemnly swear that I will support and defend the Constitution of the United States against all enemies, foreign and domestic; that I will bear true faith and allegiance to the same; and that I will obey the orders of the President of the United States and the orders of the officers appointed over me, according to regulations and the Uniform Code of Military Justice. So help me God!"

He looked at each of us and said, "Congratulations, you are now officially in the U.S. military. You are now subject to legal orders and entitled to military pay and benefits. You are dismissed to check in for boot camp."

I tried to swallow but nothing. I said a broken, "Thank you, sir," that I think sounded a lot more like, "Holy shit, what just happened?"

It was awesome, though. I was enlisted. I remember that they gave me an extra rank right outta the gates because I was an Eagle Scout. Thank God Mom made me finish that shit. I also had a clause in my enlistment contract that guaranteed me an opportunity at boot camp to screen for BUD/S.

So, when I got to boot camp, I got my shot. There's absolutely nothing in me that wanted… if the Navy SEALS had been Army SEALS, I would have gone into the Army. I couldn't have cared less what branch. I told myself, "That's the hardest thing; that's what I'm doing." Boot camp was just like this really annoying step I had to get past.

I got off the white military prison bus that picked me up at the airport in Chicago, and found myself at Navy Boot Camp, Great Lakes. Boot camp was a joke physically, but it was just miserable. It was supposed to be. It was miserable because it was like being in prison. There was a guy right there in my shit all the time. We had bunk beds like some kinda sick summer camp. We were living in close proximity with fifty or more other guys. No phone, no computer, none of that shit. Nighttime was the only time I had to myself. I couldn't even jerk off in my rack because there was a guy staying on the top bunk.

Lights out and taps was at 10 p.m. I needed to be in bed and trying to sleep because they'd wake us up at 4 a.m., usually by smashing a metal trash can down the middle of the division barracks. So, after 10 p.m. was sort of my own time, but no one really messed around because we were so tired. I usually stayed up about a half hour and read through the Bible.

I'd read the Bible because it was the only book we were allowed to have with us and thank God, too, because it brought me comfort. I mean, we could have whatever religious book we wanted, I guess. I remember getting a Spanish Bible for one of the guys in my division. The only English I ever heard him speak was, "Yes, petty officer." He joined with no green card but wanted to be a U.S. citizen. Turned out, if you joined the military, they'd fast track that shit. Talk about doing it the right way…

I had friendships there as best I could. It was kinda like survival, though. You get along with dudes because you have to. Some guys acted a bitch, though. I watched dudes lose their shit a little bit, too. They'd claim to be crazy, hoping to get shit-canned back to freedom. Guys would yell shit out like, "My recruiter lied to me," with tears streaming down their faces and whatnot. "I just wanted to go to college!" Comical shit. They're probably all out now running around with multi-cam baseball hats, beards, and K9 service dogs claiming PTSD from being wherever. Tools…

Around the second or third week, after we'd all had time to kinda unpack ourselves and let this new way of life sink in, the RDC (Recruit Division Commander) assholes took a break from yelling and started giving out jobs and asking for volunteers. I took on the responsibility of Religious Petty Officer and I would lead the entire division in prayer every night and a Bible study on Sunday. Instead of doing Navy shit work like swabbing the deck for the thousandth time, I'd go to the church. I was allowed to go to the church all day on Sunday and help the chaplains out. Many times, it just meant swabbing the deck over there. Look, I'd rather be cleaning the shitter in the church than the one in the division any day. No one messed with us over there. I'd do the little service and then I'd stay at church and go to little areas that I knew of and sleep. It's funny, too, because at the time I didn't think anyone knew, as if I wasn't the first one at Navy boot camp to find the secret sleeping spot in the back of the chapel.

The SEAL Motivators, a couple of Navy SEALs that worked with the recruits at boot camp directly, came in to talk to us around the second week. They gave this little brief and talked about naval special warfare. They were basically dicks, kind of cocky, but they talked all about special operations.

"You guys can go EOD, Diver, SEAL, or Special Boat Unit. How many of you recruits want to be SEALs?" Maybe four of us raised our hands and they were like, "Of course you do."

I remember one of them I thought was pretty cool, but I didn't know much. These were some of the first SEALs I'd ever had any kind of real contact with, like they were aliens or something. But one guy…there were these rumors…I forget his name. I think Black or something like that. But, anyway, there were rumors that he had all these knife kills in Vietnam or some shit so all of us were like, "Holy shit, this dude's a badass." There was this other asshole with a mustache…80s Tom Selleck-style. And these dudes were all big, jacked dudes that worked out every day and talked a lot of shit.

They seemed larger than life. But these guys had already been in a while and they were basically on a break. There was nothing combat-related going on when I was going through boot camp. None of these guys had really done shit, you know? Like I might hear of a guy, maybe he did an off-shore oil rig take down. In other countries, oil rigs might get taken over by terrorists and maybe have to get re-taken. So SEALs would go do it. But there was no war going on. I'd heard about Grenada and Panama. Those were the big SEAL ops, that and Vietnam, but there was nothing really going on when I joined up. So, if a dude had done anything, an op to go blow up railroad tracks somewhere in Bosnia, or whatever, the thought was, "This dude's a war hero."

They gave me a time to show up for the Physical Readiness Test (PRT). It was sit-ups, push-ups, pull-ups, a run, and a swim, all back to back. If I passed it, I got orders to BUD/S. I crushed it. Once I had passed, I was allowed to go work out with the SEAL instructors. So, every morning, an hour before everyone else got up to do jumping jacks and march in circles, I'd go over to the indoor base pool.

It was a cold walk in the dark every morning. I think the average temperature in Great Lakes in the winter topped out around fourteen degrees sometime after lunch. The SEAL Motivators would be there every morning with the same group of assholes that had passed the PRT, probably around fifty guys total. From 4 a.m. to sometime around 7 a.m., we worked out. One day was swimming; one day was running. There was always some sort of dick dragger work-out involved. Some of those guys were about to graduate boot camp, and they'd already gotten their BUD/S class date or whatever, and some guys, like me, had just started. It was funny because the guys that had been there for like eight weeks, they acted like they were already SEALs. Then I watched those same guys quit when we got to BUD/S. We'd do the PRT every Friday with the next group of new recruits that rogered up for Special Operations. But everyone had to do the PRT at least one more time after graduation from boot camp before getting final orders to class up.

I wasn't taught how to use any actual weapons in Navy boot camp. It was just marching around, getting yelled at about nonsense, and lots of folding uniforms and cleaning shit…and I was there in the winter. It was freezing. We'd stand there in the mornings just…Oh, my God, stand at attention for what would seem like hours. I mean people would fall asleep in lines and, like a domino effect, fall into the person in front of them. It was just to basically break down any resistance to not doing what you're told. It was all about discipline and endurance at that point, mostly discipline, making you somebody that listens to orders, getting you ready to go out and be on a ship. Because you can't screw up on a ship. It's a little floating city, Big Navy, you had be able to get to battle stations and fight or whatever, all this bullshit. Thank God there's people to do that job.

It was thirteen really boring weeks. In that time, I was mentally just moving more and more toward graduation. My RDCs liked me, though. I wasn't an asshole and was a hard worker. I didn't want to screw up the chance to go to BUD/S. I was going in there already thinking from a professional mindset. Most guys that wanted special programs were absolutely focused on getting there.

The rest of boot camp went on in this fashion for what seemed like years, and then one day, just like that, it was graduation. Freedom was short-lived, though. I went straight back to the airport and flew to Norfolk, Virginia. The USO at the airport got me a shuttle ride out to the Damneck Annex of Naval Air Station Oceanna, and I reported into the quarterdeck to start my "A" school. It was supposed to basically bridge the gap from boot camp to the actual Navy fleet.

Before boot camp, after I'd joined up, I had an opportunity to pick my "A" school from a list of schools that were called "source ratings" for Special Operations and Special Warfare. I tried to choose to be a corpsman, a medic. I didn't necessarily want to be a medic. I just thought, out of all the things they were offering, it sounded like it could be fun and maybe more along the lines of what I'd need to do later to be a SEAL.

When I was enlisting, they reviewed my criminal record and they were like, "Uh, you have been arrested for drugs. Obviously you've smoked marijuana."

I was like, "Yeah? Was that a question?"

"How many times?"

"I don't know. A couple hundred."

And they were like, "Jesus Christ!"

So I was given an official drug waiver to come into the Navy and I was only allowed to choose certain things. I was on a waiver for marijuana so they wouldn't let me be a medic. I aced my ASVAB so I had my pick and I just picked something else; it didn't really matter to me. I ended up choosing OSA, Operations Specialist School.

In the Navy, an operations specialist was basically the navigator on big ships, up there in the bridge wing, driving the vessel. So, for nine weeks, I learned all this bullshit to be a navigator on a big ship, and all I could think about was going to BUD/S.

I was in classrooms all day, but I had a little bit more liberty. On weekends, I was allowed to go into town but I had to wear my uniform and I looked like a Dixie Cup-wearing dick. The uniform was all white, no medals except the one National Defense medal that everyone gets for joining up. The pants were white cotton bell bottoms and I looked like I was serving ice cream in the 50s. It wasn't until about week six that I could wear actual jeans and a t-shirt instead of the uniform. I usually just stayed on base, though, jacking steel and pumping pig all day. I needed to be ready for when that shit show was over and BUD/S began.

I remember at Damneck that there were a couple of us that were going to BUD/S. We had a class number already and we would do our workouts in the mornings before class and then run on the beach in the soft sand in the evenings. I could see SEAL Team 6 down the beach and I remember I used to run as far as I could toward the compound. Guards would come out on the beach and stop me, telling me to turn back. I would stand there and just look at it. It looked really intimidating from the beach, with all the buildings. There were no windows on anything, just these massive buildings. I remember just looking at them and thinking, I'm gonna be there someday.

Sometimes I'd see guys out on that beach working out. These guys were in Green Team, SEALs who were trying out for SEAL Team 6. I remember seeing those guys just cruising by us in a little group. It was just a bunch of tattooed-out, jacked-up dudes running by on base and it was funny to me because dudes would have beards, stupid mustaches, all kinds of crazy shit, shirts off, cammie pants, and boots on. I'd never seen anything like this in the Navy. These dudes didn't look like anybody else and they didn't care. All I could think was, I can't wait until I'm at that place.

Chapter 3

TO HELL AND BEYOND

So I finally graduated from what felt like the big NAVY. I'd be leaving Damneck, hopefully to return some day and go to Green Team. I had to make it through BUD/S first. But I was already thinking SEAL TEAM SIX. Someday, I told myself. Someday I'd be there. Then I packed my shit and headed off to Coronado, California.

I felt like I was the only one on the plane. I was in my dress uniform, like an asshole. I didn't take any leave. I was only twenty years old. What was I gonna do anyway? I got there a month before my class started. I got off the plane and went to the USO in the San Diego airport. They got me a shuttle ride over to Naval Amphibious Base Coronado. By the time I showed up, it was after midnight and I remember looking for where to go. I didn't know who I was supposed to check in with and I was on the other side of the base from where I was supposed to be. I was a mess. Nobody really talked to me or told me what was going on. I had to kind of figure it out. I was just trying to find other guys that were going to be in my class.

I finally found the BUD/S quarterdeck and the king shit sitting behind the desk was a fellow BUD/S student, but you'd have thought this guy ran the place. I walked up and he was asleep in his chair behind the window and his boots were up on the desk. I knocked on the glass. He woke up and said, "Hey, bro, relax, my name's Luke. Obviously you're new here. I gotcha, bro." He said it all chill-like as if he couldn't care less. Then he bummed a dip off of me and ended up killing the last of the can.

Luke gave me directions to an open barracks where I could grab a rack because there weren't any more rooms. He didn't bother telling me anything about what to expect the next day. I rolled into the barracks and grabbed a rack. There were maybe fifteen guys in there. That small group would eventually build into upward of two hundred by the time First Phase started.

I didn't know my ass from a hole in the ground. I didn't know what was going on really. There were guys that were in my BUD/S class that had been there a couple more weeks than me. We were waiting on all these other guys to graduate from their A schools or come from wherever they were in the Navy and get there, because we had a hard start date for Day 1. Anyway, those guys were all still up getting their "greens" ready for inspection that next morning.

I got a uniform from one of the rollbacks and hit the rack. I showed up the next day and I remember my boots weren't shined up. I'd just gotten them, and had about three hours of sleep. And there we were, out there at five in the morning, having inspection. So I just threw on the cammies that I got. I had no name stenciled on anything; nothing was done. My greens weren't starched; they weren't anything. Other guys' uniforms were starched so heavy they were literally rigid. I was standing there and I remember this instructor came up to me. It was Instructor Buck. He got so close to my face that his Copenhagen breath made me want to puke. He started right in, "What's your name, FUCK FACE?"

Then he looked at my boots and I'm like, "Aww, man…"

"Lock it up!" he yelled in my face. "Because of this asshole, everybody get wet and sandy!"

So we had to run from Building 618, the barracks, out to the ocean, get wet, roll around in the sand, and run back. All I could think of was, "First morning and I got the entire class wet and sandy." I thought I was going to get kicked out of BUD/S before it even started. I felt like the whole class hated me. I felt horrible, but all I could do was laugh.

The instructors had tossed the barracks while we were out getting wet. Every single room was a disaster. We ended up making trips to the surf zone for two more hours. Back and forth, running through the sand up over the massive berms that separated the compound from the ocean. So we'd go get wet, roll around in the sand, run back, stand in line. Then next you'd see a mattress fly out the second deck. What the hell was this? Shit was flying out everywhere, dip cans were getting frisbeed along with guys' magazines, protein powder, and anything else that was loose and available to be thrown. They were starting to pile up on the pavement below.

It was chaos. Some guys were still running back from the surf. Others were already back and trying to get back in ranks. The instructors would walk over to the guys standing in ranks and yell, "Who's dip is this? Open your mouth."

Then they'd just dump the whole can of tobacco into somebody's mouth, didn't matter who. I thought it was hilarious.

Then one of them yelled, "We told you that you can't dip here."

We all dipped anyway.

Then I remember they made the whole group get in a line in push-up position. Each guy had to put his feet on the shoulders of the guy behind him. So, once everybody was in position with their feet on somebody's shoulders, we did push-ups together as a class until we couldn't physically do them anymore. The instructors told us to make walrus mating calls while we did the push-ups.

Then they made us run down to the ocean, get a mouthful of water and run back. It was like five hundred yards out to the surf because the tide was out. We also had to run up and over these huge sand berms that were piled up to break the waves from crashing into the BUD/S compound. I'd have to have a mouthful of salt water when I got back.

They'd say, "All right; spit it out."

There was always one asshole that short-changed the run out to the surf and tried to cheat. They'd usually catch him and then they yelled, "Asshole, you spit your water out already. Go back."

And he'd run off by himself, and they'd yell, "Take a swim buddy!"

So they started ingraining into us that, day one, you can never be by yourself. We actually got a swim buddy assigned in BUD/S. My first two ended up quitting. Then I got Luke as my swim buddy, the hard mofo that checked me in that first night. Luke made it through.

I was really happy to be there, even happy to go hit the surf. I thought, "This is it; I'm in BUD/S." This was my new normal, lying in the surf zone, waves crashing over me for what seemed like hours, just lying there with my class, arms locked together, freezing…

I remember we had log PT that first day, too. What a treat. It was about three hours of pure misery. Nobody was a team. Everyone was an individual. But, after standing with a telephone pole over our heads for ten minutes at a time, guys either quit or sacked up real quick and started working together. We'd have to pick the log up and right-shoulder it. Then we'd have to full-arm extension the log over our heads, then left-shoulder it. We would repeat this over and over until they told us to do sit-ups with the logs across our chests, or duck walks carrying the logs between our legs. It was nothing like anything I'd ever experienced. Guys started quitting right off the bat.

That first week introduced us to pretty much every physical evolution we would endure throughout BUD/S. Besides Hell Week, that first week of BUD/S was probably one of the worst. We had an O-course after breakfast the second day. I was so stiff and sore from the first day, I remember thinking, "Obstacle course? How is that possible?" Thank God I was 20.

We ran from breakfast at the chow hall over a mile back to the compound, through the gate and right out to the obstacle course. We ran everywhere. We ran six miles a day just to eat. It wasn't really running; it was more of a painful recovery shuffle to and from. But every evolution in BUD/S is broken up between these shuffles. It's the only waking rest we got.

I remember the boats, of course. Inflatable boats, small or IBS for short, they were called. We'd paddle out past the surf zone in these boat races, like trying to paddle a little rubber boat up Niagara Falls. Everything was a race and everything was a competition. If we made it past the breakers, we'd dump our boat, flip it back over, and try to shoot the rapids on the way back in. It was a total shit show, always. If the surf was up, there'd be boats, paddles, and BUD/S students like a gypsy camp all over the beach.

Guys that lost would be bear-crawling around the beach, getting a mouthful of water, getting a mouthful of sand, whatever, and then back to the ocean. This went on for hours, pretty much daily. It was like the boats became the filler between all the other evolutions. We had to work as a team.

We had classroom instruction, but it was all silly shit like tide theory or whatnot. Mostly they were just looking for guys to fall asleep. They'd have buckets of ice water to stick your head in. There was a boat, an IBS, outside the classroom on the "grinder," full of water and ice. They'd make you go lay in the boat if you fell asleep. Or, after enough guys fell asleep, they'd just make the whole class do fifty push-ups and run to the surf zone.

The grinder was like a big parking lot in the middle of the compound that had these little frog feet painted on the ground all over the place. We'd run there as a class to start our day at 5 a.m. or whatever. Guys would fill in, each guy on one spot, and we'd have an instructor up front on a platform. He'd get up there all fresh and lead PT while he talked loads of shit to the class about how we were all spoon-chested and our arms were buggy whips or whatever. Where these guys came up with this bullshit, I wish I knew. Some of it was pure gold. Some guys were weak and pitiful, but I was barrel-chested and my arms were pure mass. I lived in the front leaning rest.

We had three timed evolutions in BUD/S. The obstacle, or "O" course, was a three-mile ocean swim and a four-mile timed run. Every other day we would do something for a recorded time. Two failures in a row on any timed evolution would get you dropped from training. The run was the worst. It was a timed run down Coronado Beach in the sand, wearing pants and jungle boots. In the first phase, we had thirty minutes to finish; by the third phase we had twenty-eight minutes to do it in. We had to keep about a seven-minute pace in the sand with boots and pants on. So the whole class was just hauling ass. There was a little break after timed evolutions while they recorded everyone's scores. Then it was right back to the training.

I remember lying out in the surf zone at night that first week, with guys getting up and just walking out and quitting, ringing the bell. And I loved it. I was like "Hell, yeah, pussies, get the hell outta here." The ocean was a great mediator because it was the one thing no one could ever train for or get used to. There were dudes that showed up looking like altered beasts, but get them cold, wet, tired, and miserable, I don't care how hard core or how in shape they were, it didn't matter. They'd quit right then and there. BUD/S went to a whole different level of mental fortitude.

Some guys quit on the first day but, for most of the guys, there was a big quit on Wednesday morning that first week. Monday went by, Tuesday went by, Wednesday morning came and there was a group of people quitting and then nobody else really quit until Hell Week. Our Hell Week was the third week of First Phase. Really not much changed in Hell Week as far as the daily and nightly routine went. Pain and suffering were just exponentially magnified due to extreme sleep deprivation. Perhaps an amazing thing about all the chaos is that we learned, by design, to rely not only on our boat crew or swim buddy; we learned that the only way to survive was to live and breathe as a *team*.

Hell Week starts with an event called breakout. The instructors put the class in the classroom on a Sunday evening. There was pizza and a movie projector and a bunch of old army cots. I remember they showed us a movie. I was pissed, sitting there waiting for breakout because I'd heard all these guys in the class before us watched Braveheart or something like that before their Hell Week, and the instructors, those cocksuckers, put on some movie about making a porno. It had Charlie Sheen in it as a porn director, molestache and all. It was the shittiest movie I'd ever seen. It wasn't porn; it was a movie about making a porn film. Older movie. But that's what they put on just to be dicks to us. I remember thinking, "What loser actually had this in the first place?"

I went and laid down in the back of the class. I think I slept for maybe thirty minutes, kind of relaxed myself. Then the class proctor came in and said, "Hey, guys, we all need to muster up out in the grinder. We're gonna go get one more chow run before Hell Week."

We walked out and it was on. The instructors kicked off the M60s, full automatic belt-fed machine guns. Some of the instructors were throwing flash-bang grenades in these big concrete trash can-looking things that just amplified the blast. There was shit blowing up everywhere, and smoke grenades everywhere. There was all this yelling and police sirens. It was just chaos. Dudes were running into each other.

We were just trying to figure out what we were supposed to do at this point. Some instructors were yelling at us to get out to the beach. Other instructors were yelling at us to get a head count. Guys, at least in my class, naturally just started forming up in their boat crews, like find the other guys in the boat crew and let's go to the beach. And eventually everybody was out on the beach getting wet and sandy and crawling down the beach. Instructors stood on the berms just shooting M60s full auto in the middle of a Sunday night in what was basically a resort destination for everyone else on that island.

I remember crawling through these swampy low spots on the beach that were full of reeds and shit. It was nasty water that just sat there stagnant, and there were these little mites, these little beach mites that were biting my skin. They pulled that shit for a couple of hours, making us crawl along behind them through the surf, then over the beach and through the reeds and so on while they walked and laughed and shot guns. Then we started log PT on the beach. Essentially, Hell Week was what we'd been doing the last two weeks, obstacle course, running around with boats on our heads, and so on. By Wednesday, dudes were like "F*** this shit. I'm outta here." Guys were hallucinating. So they just had to basically make up games like boat races in the pool or whatever to keep guys awake. Physically the class was done.

I wouldn't even think quit. I knew I wasn't gonna quit. I would just think, I've got to take this in small chunks. It was too overwhelming otherwise. So the way to do it, at least for me, was to make it from meal to meal. So I'd have breakfast and, while I was eating, I was thinking I'm just gonna get to lunch. We're gonna go do whatever we've got, but I'm gonna get to lunch. And then I'd think about dinner. And then we'd have mid rats, meaning that sometime around midnight to one a.m., we'd get another meal.

But I remember, maybe it was the second day, I was standing in front of the chow hall waiting to get in line and I was just pissing myself, eyes closed, half asleep. And I opened my eyes and there was this instructor standing there and he was like, "Are you kidding me? This is where we eat."

He made me lay on the ground. "Sop up that piss," he yelled.

Everybody was going inside to eat and I was rolling in my own piss in front of the chow hall on the street. I didn't care. I was just rolling around in it. And the instructor, he was like, "Oh, yeah, sop that shit up." Stupid shit. I thought it was funny.

I remember I got strep throat. I lost control of my tongue and the instructors were making fun of me. One came over, one of the instructors who I was actually at Dev Group later with. Good dude. But he came over and dumped hot sauce in my mouth. Hot sauce. And I was drooling everywhere. And then he felt bad, and he goes, "Wow, your throat's really messed up. I thought you were just being a bitch." All because I asked him on Wednesday for a throat lozenge. I walked over to the instructors' table in the chow hall and I said, "I got a really bad sore throat. Can I get like a lozenge or something?" I couldn't talk right because my tongue wasn't working, and they all just dropped their forks.

"Are you kidding me, dude," they said, "It's Hell Week."

And I said, "I think there's something wrong with my throat."

And I just watched this guy get up and he said, "Sheff, sit down. Tilt your head back and open your mouth."

I did, and he just dumped Tabasco sauce in my mouth. Dudes in my class were like "holy shit." It was so bad, I was drooling everywhere. And this asshole actually told me to swallow it, swallow Tabasco.

Finally, one of the other guys comes up and said, "Let me look in your throat." I let him look at it and he said, "Damn, this guy's throat's really jacked up."

And they kind of felt bad. I washed my mouth out with some water and they actually gave me a couple of throat lozenges. At the med check later, the doc tells me, "Yeah, you got strep throat. You want to quit?"

"No," I replied.

"All right then; get back with your class."

As soon as the docs cleared me and I walked out of the medical building, there was an instructor spraying me down with a water hose to make sure I wasn't dry any longer than absolutely necessary.

Before Hell Week, I wrote a Bible verse underneath the brim of my camouflage hat. It simply read, Phil 4:13. I don't know how many times I've said those words to myself. I just know that people ask where I got the strength to pull through. And I can tell you that, when it got miserable, really miserable, I'd say to myself, *I can do all things through Jesus Christ, for it is He who strengthens me.* Saying those words is one thing. The key to the castle is to believe, and I give all glory and credit to God for making it through anything. I learned that you don't get to hold God's hand just when you want to. Not when *He* holds *you* in His.

* * *

Exhaustion, sleep deprivation and hypothermia became a regular part of my routine. It sucked, but it was also what I had been waiting for. It was the ultimate test, I thought. Sitting there at the end of the week in a hole of mud and stench, we had to look at each other and laugh a bit. As I looked around on that Friday afternoon, I couldn't help but notice the size of our class. We were down to about a quarter of what we started with and I knew everyone by name. It was a great feeling when Hell Week was secured and we were cut away to our rooms for a forty-eight hour unconscious bed-wetting contest. I called my dad and Leslie and told them I had made it.

I slept so hard that I didn't even wake up to my own piss. My body began to swell and ache. God bless my mom. She came and got me and took me to a hotel. I just faintly remember falling asleep in the rental car. Mom was dry heaving from the smell of me and trying to roll all the windows down. See, Mom had always been there for me and Hell Week was no exception.

I think I slept for almost eighteen hours. As great as the feeling of accomplishment was, I quickly came back to the reality that I had only completed three weeks of BUD/S. There were still five weeks of First Phase left. We didn't get a medal for making it through Hell Week, but we did receive something a bit more special.

The Monday after Hell Week was secured, we showed up for our medical examination and, while we were waiting to see the doctors, the entire class, one by one, received a camouflage Bible with a black Navy SEAL Trident on the front cover. This was the first thing I'd received with a trident on it from the military. When I opened it, the first page read,

Ossa Sheffield (Class #233)

Congratulations

Upon your successful completion of "Hell Week," 08-13 Oct 00

Blessings,

1 Cor 9:24 -27

Chapter 4
TEAMS AND SHIT

After my Hell Week was secured, I turned twenty-one on October 30, 2000. My birthday was spent getting wet and sandy with my swim buddy and then the whole class treading water in San Diego Bay. Then the instructors made what was left of our class sing happy birthday, while we all laid on a steel pier and jack-hammered from the cold. It was a memorable twenty-first birthday.

We finally finished First Phase after five more weeks of pain and suffering. I think my class had dwindled down to about twenty-eight guys. We all had proven we wouldn't quit, so it was time for the instructors to start teaching a skill.

Second Phase is also known as Dive Phase. Whenever you switch phases, the instructor cadre changes, too. The instructors from Dive Phase were a special breed of hateful. Physical tests and training continued, except the completion times on runs, swims, and obstacle courses were reduced. In the beginning, most of our time was spent learning dive physics and how to dive on open circuit SCUBA. Much like Hell Week, it was a major milestone to pass in First Phase, Second Phase had another major milestone called Pool Completion. Simply put, Pool

Comp was a life-saving test and required each individual to pass on his own, rather than as a boat crew or class. It is statistically responsible for the next largest group of BUD/S failures, typically bringing the attrition rate to the famous eighty percent.

During Pool Comp, we were given a series of underwater tests while wearing "Twin Eighty" dive tanks. Instructors pulled off our goggles and tied our air hoses in knots while we were underwater. The only way to pass was to meticulously fix yourself, exactly as instructed, while on an extremely long and uncomfortable breath hold. If any student re-donned his equipment out of sequence, or panicked, that student failed. We were allowed two attempts before being dropped from training. Passing out while on a breath hold, which many do, counts as an attempt. Like with everything else at BUD/S, the instructors are only looking for perfection.

Dive Phase was as much of a test on physical abilities as it was on mental ability. There was always an objective for the dive. Usually it was a target of some kind. We would go out at night in the pitch black and insert into the water off of Zodiacs (a type of inflatable boat), submerging several miles from the target. Diving into the dark water with only a swim buddy, a compass, and a stopwatch was the norm. Sometimes the instructors even let us fill our wet suits with sand before the dive.

The dives were completed successfully because of the hours of time planning and doing pace lines and accuracy dives. There's definitely a feeling of claustrophobia from being submerged for hours in the pitch-black ocean at night. Most of us got used to it. We had to. We would do a four-hour dive almost daily, followed by another one at night.

We left Dive Phase with a whole new confidence in the water that is shared by every SEAL. We spent so much time in and under the water, it became a second home.

The third and final phase of BUD/S is land warfare and is comprised of land navigation, tactics, and more shooting than the entire Marine Corps does in a year. This phase is the beginning of true soldiering, all while still getting our asses kicked with the same myriad of tests as before, just with faster times and longer runs.

This phase is the initial building block of SEAL combat training. We spent the first few weeks learning about basic weapons skills and how to properly wear our gear. We were taught first to use two primary weapons. The first was the Colt M4 5.56. This was to be my primary rifle. My secondary was a Sig Sauer P226 9mm pistol. We were timed on taking them apart, cleaning them, and putting them back together with an instructor inspection test when the time stopped. If your weapons were still dirty, it was your ass.

After some basic weapons training, we went to La Posta, California, for land navigation training. Here we learned everything about maps, compasses, and how to read terrain. The tests consisted of multiple timed land navigation courses through the mountains. The instructors gave us one grid coordinate and we had to plot the point with a protractor and use our pace and compass bearing to find the next point. If we were successful, we'd find a red ammo can attached to a tree. Inside the metal box was the next point to plot and move to. If you didn't make it through all your points in four hours, or if you didn't plot them correctly, you were given one more attempt. If you didn't make that, you were dropped from training. Believe it or not, this still happens at this point in the game.

La Posta was a bit unique for our class and one of the many reasons why Class 233 was the hardest BUD/S class of all time. We spent the last few days in the field in small teams of six. It had been snowing non-stop, which was as unusual as when it rained during our Hell Week.

Just as the weather went to full blizzard mode, the instructors came over the radio and gave us all the same surprise grid location to navigate to. As we came out of the field, we noticed something that I almost couldn't believe. They had marched us into a large open area with a frozen pond covered in snow.

The head instructor stood across the pond looking over at us.

"Okay, guys, good news. The Lord has blessed us with some amazing weather and, for the benefit of training, we need to take advantage of it. There's cold, and then there's miserable. We just want to make sure we cover the whole spectrum, so leave your clothes on and get your asses in the water."

That was a fun two hours. Our hypothermia was only suppressed by getting out of the water and doing forms of physical exertion to warm back up. My favorite was getting in a big line, starting in the push-up position. I had my hands on the ground and my feet were on the shoulders of the guy behind me. The guy in front of me had his feet on my shoulders. Slush and mud began to trickle down my face as we were told to start moving forward as a class. They walked us around on our hands in a big fire worm. I couldn't help but laugh and think about the first day of BUD/S.

After Land Navigation, we went to Camp Pendleton for two weeks. Camp Pendleton is a massive Marine base north of San Diego that consists of mountains, hills, and some wide-open spaces to shoot. Camp Pendleton is where we got proficient at shooting our weapons. Everyone strove for perfection because anything less and we were forced to do a timed Mt. Seri Bache run. That hill was ridiculously steep and the best thing was, if we didn't make it up and back in the eight minutes allotted, which was damned near impossible, we'd line up and do it again.

The sixth and seventh weeks of Third Phase were spent on San Clemente Island. Most of the time spent on "The Island" is spent on shooting, demolitions, and target assault. As a rite of passage, we learned to blow up Jap Scullys with haversacks full of explosives. It was UDT (Underwater Demolition Team) appreciation as we swam out with just knife, fins, mask, and explosives. We then rigged seven Jap Scullys to blow out of the water, like they did to clear the beaches in World War II.

The Island was also particularly scary on the night swims, where the instructors would drop us off from a boat on one side of the Island and we'd have to swim through shark-infested waters to the other side. I'm still not sure what the point of that was. When the two weeks ended and we landed back in San Diego, we were on another level. There was energy among the class, all packed into a bus heading back to the BUD/S compound. We felt like nothing could hurt us. All we had to do was make it to graduation and then the real journey begins, I thought.

When BUD/S finally ended on March 30, 2001, there was a graduation ceremony at the base in Coronado for the twenty-eight of us who had survived. It was a good feeling that day. I felt an amazing sense of accomplishment. Looking at those guys in my class, as different as we were—family, background, faith—I realized that we were far more similar than I had imagined. None of us knew what the future would hold and we didn't care. We just lived in the moment.

Shortly after graduation, we were sent to Fort Benning, Georgia, for three weeks of Basic Parachute Training. One of the instructors was a short Army guy with "Little Man" syndrome and he said, "Listen up, I own the 'A' in SEAL. A is for air, in case you limp dicks haven't figured it out yet. *Sea, Air, Land*. Bet that surprises some of you, huh?" I was thinking, "Wow, What a douche-bag!"

A nutless monkey can static line out of an airplane and this dipshit was acting like he was God's gift to the military. If I had heard him say that he was elite one more time, I could've thrown up in my mouth.

Jump school was a joke. They take three weeks to teach you how to run out of the airplane. The parachute opens automatically. We did two weeks of running around and listening to asshats talk, and then we got to do five jumps in week three. That was it. Congratulations! You can fall out of an airplane!

After jump school, we went through another training course called SEAL Qualification Training, or SQT. Real combat training started here. SQT was a familiarization. They took me from a BUD/S student and made me a Navy SEAL so I could go into a platoon and have an idea how to wear the gear, how to shoot, how to move. It was basically a condensed Platoon work-up.

Six months later, we graduated and I was only two weeks away from my first SEAL Command. Really, the only significant thing between SQT and my first SEAL Team was that I got married.

I went home on leave, drove from San Diego, California to San Angelo, Texas straight to my girlfriend's house. I picked her up and I drove out to this place by the lake where I used to run to get ready for BUD/S. I didn't get on a knee or anything. I just handed her a little black flip-open box. That's about as romantic as I got. She opened it, then started crying.

Leslie had dreams of becoming a missionary in Russia. She was on a track scholarship as well. She left all of it to tag along with me into the Navy. We went to the courthouse and filed the paperwork and planned a hasty wedding at the church for September 15, 2001. Four days before the wedding, the towers fell in New York City. My brother joined the Navy the following week.

We were already married, on paper anyway, and I told her, "Whatever we're gonna be doing, we're gonna continue together. I'm a new guy anyway; it's not like they're gonna be asking for all the new guys from BUD/S to mount up and go to war."

I actually thought they might call me personally, though.

We got married and it was a beautiful wedding. Leslie had just had knee surgery from playing volleyball, but you couldn't tell it when she walked in. She lit up the church. She was beautiful. We kinda blocked everything else out for a few moments that day and it was really special. The place looked amazing, no thanks to me. She had planned everything with the help of some close friends and family. My two youth pastors married us; it was a tag team effort. Mills and Kevin have always been special people to us and I know they lost sleep praying personally for me through the years. We got married at the Baptist church we both went to. Hearts were breaking all over the place.

Our honeymoon was driving to Virginia Beach. The wedding was great, everything was good, the stress was different than normal; there were a lot of questions. Everyone in the church wondered, "9/11 just happened. You're a Navy SEAL. Do you think you'll go?" I had no answers.

I was hoping we would go. I was twenty-one, a Navy SEAL and by all accounts America was going to war. I reported to SEAL Team Eight five days after getting married.

I showed up to check in, wearing my dress uniform, and the guys working the quarterdeck duty, also SEALs, were like, "Oh, shit, new meat, huh? Drop down and push 'em out."

So I was doing push-ups in my dress uniform and my chief happened to be walking down the hallway. He didn't even skip a beat when he said, "Hey, dipshit, go change or you're just gonna keep getting messed with."

I guess I half-expected lots of pats on the back for making it through that grueling program, but nobody cared. I didn't even have a trident yet. I'd just gone through this hellacious experience of BUD/S and SQT, but they didn't care. They'd all been through BUD/S. That was my read-in to SEAL Team Eight.

"Congratulations, you made it through BUD/S. So has everyone else here. None of us think you're special. Now keep your suck hole shut and ears open and you might learn something, new meat!"

I didn't care, though. Showing up to that SEAL Team finally, I felt like I was on top of the world.

First day I went into my platoon and looked around. Those dudes were pretty big—everybody was into lifting heavy—pre-Taliban. Back then, before the wars, it was all about how much weight you could bench press and squat. Then we started going to war and realized we needed to be able to run a marathon. All my guys still benched over five hundred pounds and could squat Eric's mother. We all had Austrian tree trunks for legs.

Later that first morning, when the platoon had assembled, my platoon chief asked if any of us were married. Several guys raised their hands, including me, and he asked for details.

"Really, Sheff? You're married? When did you get married?"

I was very proud, probably beaming. I said, "On September 15, Chief."

He looked at me in horror. "Are you kidding me? You got married a week before you showed up? And how old are you? Twenty-one? Wow, you are one simple dumb ass, aren't you? We'll call this your practice wife."

After the morning word for the platoon, one of the guys took me around and got me checked into the command. First stop was supply. Piles of gear, bags of gear, the initial new guy Navy SEAL gear issue. Wet suits, fins, different cammies for different weather, different kit, water, jungle, flotation, Kevlar, I mean everything I could imagine. It was like Christmas. It was a long first couple of weeks that took some getting used to.

I always involved Leslie in what was going on. Wives were always a part of it when they could be; it was the only way to handle that lifestyle successfully. Most of the time, though, as long as I wasn't being an asshole, Leslie was totally cool with me hanging with the bros. Those guys were a second family and the hard truth is that we ended up spending more time with teammates than spouses. We had to. We'd be going through a year-and-a-half worth of training together day in and day out and then deploy somewhere for six months.

There was a structure to the platoon. There was one commissioned officer—the Officer in Charge (OIC), an O3 lieutenant-type—but the chief usually gave the orders. Non-commissioned officers in the Navy are called petty officers, E4 through E9. An E4 is a third-class petty officer. An E5 is a second-class petty officer. An E6 is a first-class petty officer. An E6 in the Navy was a big deal and, in the Teams, they were generally the leading petty officer (LPO) of a platoon. The LPO ran the day-to-day operations of platoon life—he was middle management. Above him was the chief, an E7. He ran the platoon. He ran everything. Final say rested with the OIC technically, but the real yes or no came from the chief.

Here's what it took to be an officer in the military: a college degree. It didn't make anyone a leader. We were lucky to have a good officer. Just because a guy was an officer didn't mean anything tactically. He could be a total shit show on target or just a complete scumbag. But, at least in the Teams, all SEAL officers went through the same BUD/S I went through.

Now there were some pretty exceptional human beings who became officers. Just don't think General George Washington, or that these guys got out on a horse with their men. Some officers would occasionally roll on the ground with us, but they would have a com guy with them. They weren't stepping foot into the target compound unless it went to shit outside and we had to bring them in to safety. It was kind of this caravan of people we had to protect because they always had their heads up each other's asses.

Under that were the Sled Dogs, E4s and E5s, guys still learning, maybe in charge of a department. I had ordinance and engineering, meaning I was responsible for all the engines for the Zodiacs, for example. I was responsible for making sure they were washed, serviced, and ready to go. Everybody had his own department. The breachers are in charge of breaching gear and the ordering and building of explosives. They maintain everything from Quickie-Saws to drills and torches. There would be a guy who was in charge of vehicles, another collateral duty—any vehicles issued to our platoon: trucks, Humvees, vans, whatever.

Work-up started right away and we were gone on the road, training constantly. It was training for everything that would be under the umbrella of a SEAL Team's responsibility. We started with diving and then rolled into close quarters battle, land warfare, urban warfare, breaching, jumping, and so on.

Eventually, during that training cycle, we covered all the training objectives in our wheelhouse, and I was just about out of my skin waiting for deployment. I had been in the Navy more than two years at this point, and I hadn't been in any combat. I knew guys that joined the Air Force who were coming home from their second deployment "over there."

Deployment time finally rolled around and we were already engaged as a country on two war fronts. I thought for sure we'd be going to Operation Enduring Freedom and boy, was I wrong. We went to Colombia, where I was tasked to teach shooting and jungle warfare to the booger eaters in the Amazon. I was from West Texas. I knew zero things about the jungle. I couldn't wait to go to war.

After six months in South America, I came home with not one cool story from that deployment. It was a booze cruise. I was almost embarrassed. We trained booger eaters the whole time. The only thing I got out of that deployment, in fact, was orders to sniper school. My chief was a sniper and I told him I was interested. I guess I made a good impression on deployment because, when we got home, they gave the platoon a list of schools that were available before the next work-up started. My name was already on the list for snipers.

Sniper school was a six-month, two-part course that encompassed more than long-range shooting. Before we ever got to take a shot, we had to learn how to hide. Stalking taught us to sneak up on an enemy undetected, and within range of a kill shot. We'd start in a field and were given a few minutes to cammie up. When the instructor told us to go, we had two hours to get up to a position within two hundred yards of the target and take an undetected shot. If the instructors saw us through their binoculars at any time during that movement, they'd have the "walker" come and kick us off the field. Two failures and you were done; go home. So we learned how to become the earth. Those who were still around after two months of stalking continued through a four-month shooting course that was second to none. We learned everything there was to know about shooting people at long ranges with multiple calibers and in all conditions.

The bullet rises a little bit when it comes out of the barrel. It doesn't go in a straight line. So, for example, with a 5.56 round at 25 yards, my bullet impact is the same as it is at 300 yards because the round comes out, crosses this medium at 25 yards, goes up and crosses it again coming down at 300 yards. That was for one specific round. We'd shoot countless rounds at different distances and note the performance of every one. We learned to build dope charts with come-ups already on them. We'd print them out and tape them to specific rifles, because each rifle shot a little different. We learned to call and hold for wind, too. The longer the shot, the more the elements affected the round. Elevation, barometric pressure, temperature, density altitude, barrel twist, and spin drift all matter.

Density altitude is universal. It doesn't matter where you are. It's the actual elevation that the bullet thinks you're at in reference to sea level. And, if it's a day full of precipitation, like the air is charged with moisture, your round is actually going to fly faster, flatter, and farther. It's the opposite of what you would think. If you shoot in the rain, rain drops aren't actually hitting the bullet. There's a cone of air that it actually moves through and thus is less affected by air with moisture.

Spin drift accounted for the actual curve in the trajectory that the round would take from the time it left my barrel until it impacted the target. For example, with an American or NATO rifle, the rifling in the barrel twists to the right at a certain rate. I know that, when the round comes out, it's going to spin to the right, so this must also be accounted for.

We used to put rounds in the fridge and on top of our truck's hood after we'd been driving for a while, and then we'd shoot them. This was to test the powder and see what the difference was at different temperatures. We had to know all of this. I could be sitting on a base at sea level, my guns sighted in at the range where it was nice and warm, and then get on a helo and climb up to twelve thousand feet with ice and snow everywhere, and still be responsible for making the shot in those conditions.

When we needed to make a shot for life and death, all those elements mattered. We had to be sub-minute accurate out to one thousand yards. For ease of math, one minute of angle is one inch at one hundred yards. At one thousand yards, it becomes ten inches. The slightest deviation in any of these calculations at that range would guarantee a miss by nearly a foot. Very few people in the world are actually snipers, but that term gets thrown around a lot by a lot of organizations. Most of them couldn't snipe a deer at the feeder.

I finished SEAL Sniper School as top stalker, and me and my shooting buddy got top shooter pair. After sniper school, I joined my second platoon already four months into its work-up and finished the training cycle in preparation for my first deployment to Afghanistan. They were in Fallon, Nevada doing tactical vehicle driving and mountain warfare training. At that time, in San Diego, California, Seal Team Six was holding tryouts for the next year's selection class, what they called Green Team.

Seal Team Six held only two tryouts annually for Green Team. One is held at Damneck, Virginia for the East Coast Teams, and one in San Diego, California for the West Coast Teams. I had missed them on the east coast during sniper school, so I asked my chief for a favor, and drove from Fallon, Nevada with my sniper teammate back out to Naval Amphibious Base, Coronado. It was the first time I'd been back since my BUD/S graduation. They were holding the tryouts at the BUD/S compound and, as I walked across that familiar grinder to check in, I remember thinking, "How did I get back here?"

The next three days I spent trying for a chance to just try out for the most elite unit in the world. The screening test was a beefed-up version of the PT test I took to get into BUD/S. Instead of a 500-meter swim, it was a mile-and-a-half swim, twenty pull-ups, one hundred push-ups, one hundred sit-ups, and a three-mile timed run, all back to back for time. Several guys failed that test. It was a physical thing just to get in. Those of us who passed were put in the old BUD/S classroom. Talk about a shitty feeling.

Some psychologist came in, introduced himself, and handed out what looked like a SAT test. He gave us all this big questionnaire, two hundred questions. After the test, he called us in one at a time and we were interviewed. There were several seasoned operators in the room. They asked me all kinds of things, made a few notes, thanked me for my time and dismissed me. Then I got back in the car with my buddy and we drove the eight hours back out to Fallon, silently going over our answers in our minds, wondering how we did on the most important interview in our lives. I didn't find out until just before we left for deployment that we had both screened positive and would get orders to Green Team '05.

We hit the deck in Bagram and before long we were in it. We were going into villages and looking for bad guys, but not one shot was ever fired. I was in Kunar a lot, which was very mountainous, like the Himalayas. We flew in Blackhawks, snow everywhere, and fast rope onto the target. We didn't do a lot of patrolling or walking far distances. Nobody really knew what they were doing yet. This was end of 2004, beginning of 2005, and guys were still figuring out how to fight the Taliban. Nobody in the military really had trained hard core in the mountains.

We were still using Vietnam tactics over there, doing the best we knew how to do. We'd land, and me and another guy might clear three compounds by ourselves. Thank God nothing bad happened, because it would've been a mess. Some days we'd have the entire village lined up. We'd have a source with us, a dude in a mask, usually some muj we were supposed to trust, to help us out.

It wasn't a very good way to do it, but it was the best way we had. We didn't have a lot of intel; we didn't have the kind of tools I would have later at DEVGRU. We used mostly HumInt—Human Intelligence—to drive our targeting. It really just meant some asshole from out of some village saying, "Hey, there's bad guys here." We would take them with us if they had been vetted and cleared, and we'd go in and try to find the Taliban.

Not one shot was ever fired at us. And we did some really stupid things I would never think about doing now. We just didn't know any better. There were a lot of guys, in fact most guys, who had no combat experience other than some story about how they *almost* got shot at. We were completely exposed, and the Teams paid for some hard lessons with blood in those early days.

But we were fast learners.

Chapter 5
GOING PRO

"Holy shit, look at this place," I thought as I rolled up to the outer gate of the Naval Special Warfare Development Group. That's the official Navy command name. Seal Team Six or simply "The Command," is how we referred to it. I always preferred the old Marcinko title Mobility Unit Six (MOB VI). I was twenty-five and had just finished my required two platoons in the regular SEAL Teams. The guard checked my ID card.

"Sheffield, Justin…yep, you're good, man," he said, waving me through to a series of barricades and more gates.

I stepped out of my truck and a few parking spaces away another SEAL stepped out of his. It was Shane. He was from the west coast. My impression of West Coast Team guys was not the best. Shane helped to change my mind, though. He was good to go and ready to throw down. He was cocky, but a solid dude.

A mutual friend I hadn't seen since BUD/S introduced me to him. The three of us stood there and looked through the fence. It was awesome. It looked like something you'd see at NASA Space Center. There were vast six-story buildings with tiny thin horizontal windows, too high to look out or into. I could hear automatic gunfire in the distance from one of the many gun ranges.

CHOP-CHOP-CHOP-CHOP-CHOP. We looked up as three little birds—MH6s—buzzed past overhead with operators hanging off the side-struts, rifles in hand. One of them looked down at us and flipped us off. We all laughed and immediately returned the gesture of endearment.

We got to our assigned gear cages and started changing out of our starched cammies and getting dressed into PT gear. There was already a mountain of gear bags to go through and sort out.

This was day one of an eight-month selection program that weeds out seventy percent of BUD/S graduates—combat-tested Navy SEALs—who attempt it. The physical and mental strain we faced was unlike anything I'd ever experienced. And every single day was your last day unless you could prove otherwise. At five minutes to 0600 on day one, the only thing we knew was the physical readiness test was first. Beyond that was a mystery. We spent the next eight months in a chaotic blunder of training and selection. If we screwed up anything, we were gone.

"First things first, fellas. Get your PT gear on and get ready for the PRT."

If we failed this physical test, we would be dropped on the spot. The PRT was a back-to-back physical tryout and began with a mile ocean swim followed by a minimum of fifteen pull-ups, ninety sit-ups and a hundred push-ups with zero rest. Last was the five-mile timed run. All of these evolutions were timed. You fail the time, you fail selection. Believe it or not, a couple of guys failed. It was embarrassing. Next, the wonderful cadre introduced themselves and broke the class into smaller teams to get us familiar with how the Assault Teams operate.

Gold Dust and Johnny, among others, were our primary cadre and would be with us through training.

The first few days of Green Team were spent checking in and sorting through a full load-out of gear. My gear cage was a monumental heap of unorganized equipment and combat gear. Everything was new. Not one item we received had ever been used before, and it was all Gucci shit.

Our first training trip was HALO/HAHO (High Altitude Low Opening, High Altitude High Opening). We went out to the hot-ass desert in Arizona. This type of insertion, and our maritime ability, were among the multiple skillsets that separated us from literally everyone else on the planet.

When we arrived at the training facility, we all poured into the large classroom and took seats. This is where all the jump briefs would go down. Many of us had hundreds of sky dives already but nothing like what we were about to do. Gold Dust, a seasoned operator and Green Team instructor in his late thirties sporting a partial beard and faded Navy tats, stood at the front of the class with Johnny and said, "Okay, fellas, the solo fun jumps are complete. This will be your first stack jump here in Green Team. Keep in mind we got some assaulters from Blue Team with us and they will be joining us on the aircraft today. We're doing a standard dive exit. HAHO profile. Tandem and Bundles will go out first. Blue Team, you guys good with that?"

I looked over and saw nods and thumbs up from the bearded Team guys at the back of the room. Then Johnny pipes up, "Guys, pay attention when you get out. Proper pull sequence. Stack up quickly and keep your heads on a swivel. We're the only Team in the world that actually uses this method of insertion, so we need proficiency. You may find yourself doing this for real sooner than you think. Make sure you check the boards outside for your stick order and cypress settings. Double check it."

We were all quiet and a bit anxious maybe. Gold Dust surveyed the room and then he asked, “Questions? Guys, I can tell a lot of you are nervous about HAHO. Let me put your minds at ease. Chicks and faggots do this on the weekends. Don’t be a pussy. Good to go?”

We all nodded.

“Okay. Now stand up. All right, gents, walk me through it. Proper pull sequence and safeties.”

We all immediately stood up and went through our sequence together as a class.

“One thousand, two thousand, look thousand, pull thousand…Arch, check, check.”

“Pull, pull at the proper altitude, never sacrifice altitude for stability.”

“Malfunction…”

“Look red, grab red, look silver, grab silver. Pull drop, pull drop, arch, check check.”

Once we finished the safety brief, guys started gathering their things and got ready to head outside for the night’s evolution.

Johnny yelled over the commotion. “All right, gents, you guys are dismissed. Get jocked up and get two JMPIs before boarding the bus.”

We all had about enough time to shove down a power bar and take an anxiety-driven power shit. I walked outside and the smell shifted from meat-eating sewage to the smell of JP8 jet full from the C130 already turning on the runway. Guys were getting jocked up with their gear on. I could see Medlow already doing stair climbs up the tower with a two-hundred-pound dummy on his shoulder.

“What is he doing?”

Shane replied as he tightened his chest strap. “Can’t follow instructions, I guess. Gonna get himself shit-canned the first trip.”

“Better him than me,” I said.

I looked at Shane. “You ready, bro?”

“Yeah, man, but I gotta take a shit now.”

I walked over to Gold Dust.

"What's your name, Sheffield?" he asked. "You've got a misrouted rifle strap. That's a safety violation. You see that fuck stick Medlow up on the tower. You're up next and be fast about it because we don't have a short bus to pick you two retards up with. Pull each other's heads out."

Johnny yelled at the class from the bus, "Bus leaves in 10! Load up!"

Everybody finally got loaded up on the bus and headed out into the darkness to the flight line. The C130's engines were getting louder as the bus approached and I flipped my NVGs down and turned them on. Some guys were quiet. Some wouldn't shut the hell up. We loaded up on the bird and packed it in like sardines. I closed my eyes once I could feel the bird airborne and took a huge puff off my O2. Then I started praying to myself and I must have fallen asleep, because the next thing I can remember was *CLAP CLAP CLAP!* This came from the lead jump instructor getting our attention.

"RAMP!"

We were coming into the release point. Gold Dust stood in the middle of the open ramp and got our attention by clapping. We could see the horizon pitch behind him as the plane rolled into its turn onto final approach for the drop. He pointed to his wrist and then held up three fingers and yelled, "3 minutes!" but we could barely hear him over the roar of the engines and the rush of air coming in.

"Stand up!"

We all helped each other up in the cramped space, doing our best to not accidentally pull our ripcord handle or worse, someone else's. That would be devastating at a time like this. The chute would deploy inside the aircraft, ripping the jumper and anyone else in the way out of the plane. A situation like this is typically unrecoverable.

We checked each other's pins to make sure they were still fully seated, and then formed up a line. I looked up toward the ramp and could see Gold Dust on a knee, lips pursed, NVGs down, looking out the side of the ramp spotting the drop zone, zero fear.

Gold Dust held up his index finger and passed over comms, "One minute!"

We all repeated the gesture up and down the line, making sure everyone was aware.

I took a deep breath in, followed by a long exhale.

"Thirty seconds, tandems and bundles standby…"

This was it. This is the moment in time where I just accepted what was ahead and let the fear exhale out of me. As the light turned from red to green, I felt the aircraft trying to stabilize as jumpers dove out. I ran down the center of the aircraft in what felt like an earthquake as the plane shifted. The guys in front of me disappeared and I took a split second to square my stance on the edge of the ramp and dive.

Arch.

One thousand, two thousand, look thousand, pull thousand was my count as I clenched my ripcord handle and punched it out of the loop, blasting the pack tray open. Looking over my right shoulder, I could see my pilot chute spring off my back and the lines unraveling as it filled with air. It sounded like fifty trash bags exploding as it violently opened.

I focused my night vision and checked my GPS and altimeter. I was in the air, floating through the pitch-black sky, unable to see a thing. My biggest concern at that moment was that there were another twenty guys falling with me, in dangerously close proximity and that, if I collided with any one of them, or worse, got wrapped up in someone else's canopy, my chances of survival were pretty slim.

I looked over to my left and saw a stack forming that looked like a stair-stepped line of parachutes silently floating through the night sky. I maneuvered over and fit myself in. It looked like a dogfight for a few minutes until it formed up complete.

There was no time to enjoy the scenery or the curve of the earth. We were all moving together at about a hundred miles an hour and one mistake would have been fatal.

Thirty minutes and twenty-five-thousand feet later, my eyeballs had finally thawed out from being frozen and my hands hurt so bad from the cold that I could've thrown up. All of us landed where we were supposed to. After the jump, there was no time to talk as we had only a few minutes to repack our parachutes and get our asses back on the plane for another turn. We did this multiple times, every day and night, for three straight weeks.

After three weeks of skydiving, we packed our gear and flew to Mississippi. The next block of training was Close Quarters Battle, or CQB. MOB VI operators become masters at this, and we spent thousands of hours on gun ranges and in "kill houses" until we became masters. CQB is extremely intense and violent with little to no room for error. This particular block of training is responsible for most all the failures that send guys back to the regular Teams.

We would start out every day with a dick dragger ten-mile run, sometimes even do it with kit on. On the days we didn't, we'd have fight club for two hours. Shane and I always squared off together and obviously Shane always got his ass beat.

Johnny took us on the first run and shit talk had started early. "Let's go, fellas. Where is Adam's fat ass? If that sack of shit falls behind one more time, I'm gonna send him home."

An hour later, we shuffled back to the training area where we lived, ate, and trained. The class was split in half and we'd go to the kill house until lunch while the other half of the class would be at the range.

The place looked like a junk yard, with long buildings connected together made out of stacked railroad ties. They all had catwalks with big A-frame tin-covered roofs, like old converted barns. They contained multiple rooms, hallways, and doors in various maze-like fashion.

Training day one, me and Shane were jocked up in full kit. We stepped up to the door of the kill house. Johnny yelled down from the rafters, "Game on, gents, first run of the day. Let's try to make it to lunch without getting shit-canned."

They made it easy to fail, too. The kill house was like being inside a shooting gallery that was constantly being reconfigured, and we had ten instructors spread out on catwalks above us watching our every move, not to mention the ever-present video cameras recording every mistake. It started small; we'd work on just one room at first. Everything from the way you turned the door knob to what foot you decided to step into the doorway with first was judged and recorded. The instructors would go over a scenario with us, then let us walk through it once. Then we damned well better be able to teach it, because there is no do-over.

"First four check in from the rear!" Johnny yelled down from the catwalk as the rest of the instructors piled up the stairs to watch us make entry into the first room.

"Medlow ready."

"Culpepper ready."

"Shane ready."

"Sheffield ready."

Gold Dust yelled, "House is ready; house is hot!"

We moved as a line up to the door and set up to make entry.

Gold Dust held us up, "Awe, look at you two lovers up front. Hang on. Hey, Adams, has your fat ass recovered from the run yet? Switch out with Shane."

Johnny looked down at us. "Anytime, gents. Get in the room."

Adams opened the door and threw a crash in too far. From the rafters the instructors all yelled, "Three f-ing feet! How many times…"

As soon as the crash exploded, my ears rang and I flew into the room and went to my spot, blasting multiple targets in the head and chest. The room was ablaze with gunfire as we blasted all the targets in seconds and called clear. Then we moved aggressively to the next room. I loved this. It was definitely not a place for pussies.

Every house run is a test. Johnny literally had pre-purchased plane tickets for the whole class every day because they knew they'd lose more than half the guys at some point in this block of training. They would turn what SEALs learned in the regular Teams and elevate it to a science and an art. The Department of the Navy spent nearly twenty million dollars turning just one of us into a DevGroup Operator. Simply put—we had to be perfect.

Every room we entered could've been our last if we messed up in training, and definitely our last if we messed up in battle. It was chaos. I absolutely loved it. I loved the pace and violence of it.

Then, about half way through CQB, we got some really bad news. The instructors told us about Operation Red Wings. We were all sick to our stomachs. We actually had to stop training for the day. All of us had friends on that bird or on the ground. This at the time was the worst single loss the SEAL Teams had ever suffered. There was only one call I wanted to make. My brother was an EOD guy at SEAL Team Eight, my old Team. I called him immediately.

"Hey, bro, I guess y'all heard?"

Brian said, "Yeah, man, it really sucks. I know those guys were in BUD/S with you."

"One is still missing," I said.

"I know, man. We've been praying. How's Green Team going?" he asked.

"I'm still here," I told him.

"You totally suck, bro, at literally everything," he chuckled.

Shane yelled from the other room. My brother heard him and said, "Oh, shit, so Shane's still there, too."

"Yeah, he's still here," I replied.

Shane walked in. "Still here…? You kidding me, bro? Of course I'm still here."

"All right, man," Brian said. "Well, I love you, bro; keep praying for us and I'll call you in a couple days."

I hung up with my brother and tried to get my mind re-focused.

We lost over half of the guys in this block of Selection. By the time we got through CQB, we could do it in our sleep.

Next was land and urban warfare, where we learned skillsets to help our small groups take on exponentially larger threats. More extensive training followed as we worked on vehicle interdiction, hand-to-hand combat, a wide range of maritime operations, more shooting, more jumping, more non-stop madness. I loved every bit of it. We all got closer as brothers and teammates.

In November of 2005, after almost eight months at Green Team, I graduated with what was left of my class, about twenty-five operators. Shane had become one of my closest friends, and he and I would be going to Blue Team together.

Chapter 6
MOB VI

I headed up to the second deck and, for the first time, I stepped foot into what would be my home for the duration of my naval career. We all walked in with cases of beer and sat down around the boardroom table.

I looked around the room. There was a badass-looking bar in the back with hanging mugs that had dudes' nicknames on them. There were operator pictures of the old days covering the walls. In the back of the room was a glass case mounted to the wall. Inside was a faded and tattered skull-and-crossbones flag. That flag means a lot of things to a lot of people but, to us, it was more of an identity. To me, the skull meant Golgotha (Hill of the Skull) where Jesus was crucified, and the crossbones signified the cross. That's what that flag originally meant for the Crusaders who came up with it. That's it. We were predominantely Christian and we fought exclusively against Muslims who hate Christians. It was a perfect fit for my happy ass.

No one said a word. We all just looked at each other in a congratulatory silence. I could damned near hear guys' hearts beating in the room. It was an awesome silence. We all knew we'd made it this far, but we still had a lot to prove.

A door from the head shed office slid open and Sonny walked out. He would be my new troop chief. He had a quiet, respectful, even humble demeanor that we all looked up to.

"First of all, I want to congratulate you for making it through Green Team. You are now part of what is arguably the best group of SEAL operators we've got. I have some thoughts, ideas, and lessons that I'm going to share with you. I consider them very important and I have tried to live by these ideals for the past eighteen years. I haven't always got it right, but I've always tried my best, and I expect no less from you."

"Here at SEAL Team Six, we do two things: We kill terrorists and we rescue hostages. That's all we do, and it's all we have to do, because no one does it better than us, and no one comes even close.

"I often speak in climbing analogies because it helps me get my point across. As a troop chief, I choose the mountain we're going to climb. It's my job to make sure you have the right gear and the proper training to get to the top of the mountain. My team leaders will strategize and pick the route, but everyone does his part to get us to the top. Once we summit, we will return to the valley, and we'll party hard, but not so hard that we're going to piss off the villagers. Then we get ready to do it all again. I live by the work hard, play hard rule. When it's time to work, you do it right the first time. When it's time to play, the beer always tastes better if the work was done right.

"The road ahead is not about you or me, but about the Team. Pay attention. Complacency kills and common sense is definitely not common. This is not about me or you. It's about your teammate. Your fire Team. Your Team. Your troop. Your squadron. Your command. And your community. In that order. Know the job of the person above you and learn what to do. But, most importantly, what not to do. Because some day you'll be taking that position.

"I don't have all the answers, but someone around here always does.

Find that person and get your answer. Also, don't be silent. Silence is consent. Speak up; be heard.

"If you want to bitch about something, and I'm sure you will eventually, go ahead. But, after five minutes, let it go. You've been heard. Maybe some good will come of it, maybe not, but it's time to move on.

"You are masters of your own destiny and you need to operate on three battlefields. The first is at home with your family; the second is here at the base; and the third is in the theater of war. The tactics in all three differ. Pick your battles wisely. Not all are worth fighting. If you remember that, you will develop good relations with your fellow SEALs and your entire support Team.

"Remember to respect the people around you. There is a clear hierarchy, absolutely, but don't make the mistake of thinking you're better or more important than the next man or woman. We are all valuable. We all need each other.

"If you have an issue with someone, try to put yourself in their shoes and then talk to them face to face. Endless emails and requests don't cut it. Go find the guy.

"Please be good to your families. Life is full of challenges, but we can deal with them.

"This is the top of the food chain, gentlemen. Perfection is elusive, but I strive for it every day, every minute of the day, and I expect you to do the same.

"Finally, remember that good is never good enough to be here."

I left that first meeting feeling pretty unreal, and it soon became apparent that operators at this command were truly different. We were treated with respect. We were told to think for ourselves. And we were trusted at a level none of us had experienced previously. For example, we each had our own cage where we kept our equipment, and I was in charge of my own gear, my weapons, my ammo. In other words, I was in control of my own destiny there and was given freedom with enough rope to hang myself. It was Big Boy Rules. We were accountable for everything now.

During the first week that I was there, I remember being in my cage well after dark, and I had stayed at work to get all my gear sorted out. It was overwhelming at first because I had all this gear and very little direction on how things needed to be. I had gear lists laid out and I was like, “Okay, my water jump bag needs wet suit, flotation. I’m gonna jump out of an airplane with this into the water and then I’ll change into this bag to do the ship attack.”

I was sitting there working on my gear at ten o’clock at night. A couple of the new guys were still up there. Sonny came over and dragged a chair out of my cage, pulled it out, and sat down. He was sitting there watching me fumble around with my kit and he’s just… “How you doing, man? How’s everything going? You married? You got any kids? Do you? Yeah. How you looking with your gear, bro? You got any questions?” He was just calm.

I was like, “Yeah, I’m not really sure how to set it up.”

He said, “Hang on,” went and grabbed his kit and dropped it in my cage.

He said, “Well, you’re new. I gotta have my shit a little different because I’m the troop chief, but here’s how I keep my radio.” He was just showing me his gear and I was looking at mine.

I muttered, “Okay, that makes sense to me. I’m probably going to be a breacher, though, so I need a pouch back here. What do you guys use?”

“Well, we’re using this now, so try this pouch back there.”

And it was like that. This guy had almost twenty years in the Navy already. He had gotten to Dev Group in the nineties. And he was taking the time to just chill out with me for a minute.

He said, "Look, man, if you have any questions—ever—come grab me and we'll sort it out. Don't just keep this unanswered question in your head. We've got too much shit going on around here."

We hit the ground hard and fast. I thought Green Team training was intense. The Assault Teams moved at a pace that was second to none. I've trained with damned near every other unit in the world and not one even came close.

My first Team leader, though, Ol' Dick Van Dickle, was a complete shit-pile bully, but the one thing that asshole did was make me lead jumper for the Team. That just meant I'd be leading in the stack during HAHO operations. I hated jumping but loved the idea of being the first one out of the plane. This decision also forced me to jump my ass off to maintain a level of perfection.

Those early days were great. The commanding officer at the time was another load, but the next four would turn out to be top-notch leaders during our nation's bloodiest combat. There's war-time leaders and peace-time leaders. These guys rent space at the command, kinda like elected officials with term limits.

We got up on step with training and I remember thinking how much faster the pace was, even from Green Team. Rolling with the squadron was game on. My shit had to be tight always. And it was. We would hammer out combat scenarios like the NFL works on plays. Day and night. Over and over. We could've been removed for performance at any time during training. We had to earn our spot there daily as new guys.

Me and Leslie spent as much time together as we could. Six months into Blue Team, it was already time for deployment. Most of the Team was going to Iraq. I'd be going back to Afghanistan. This deployment would be different, I hoped.

Deployment day came and we all got dropped off at the fence. Our wives weren't allowed on the compound for anything outside of an emergency, which was as it should be.

I looked at Leslie. "Hey, you okay, Babe? Just a walk in the park. I'll be back."

"I know," she said. "This just came up quick, I guess. It just hit me. I love you."

"Love you, too. I'll call you when I can. Pray for us, Babe. God's got us."

"I know, Babe, and I will," she said, wiping tears off her face and trying to be strong. We said a prayer together, then I hugged her and kissed her goodbye.

I rolled into the Team room and I could see stacks of wills, powers of attorney, and Casualty Assistance Calls Officer (CACO) forms laid out on the long tables in the middle of our room. There was a representative from each department making sure we had all our paperwork straight. We'd have to sign our wills and CACO sheets, which was basically planning our own funerals. We'd write down details like who'd carry the casket, what music we wanted played, where we wanted to be buried, and so on. Some guys were so squared away they had thumb drives with everything already done, pictures and all.

Over the confusion, I heard the CO pipe up, "All right, guys, listen up, JAG is gonna put out the ROE (rules of engagement) brief!"

We all took our seats and some guys leaned on the desks that stretched around the perimeter of the room.

"You're allowed to engage the enemy if they show hostile act or hostile intent… That means you do not have to wait until you're being shot at to engage someone. If the enemy is moving to high ground or if it looks like they're maneuvering and not surrendering, you're allowed to engage."

"Yeah, thanks, sir, we got it."

Sonny, the troop chief, walked to the front of the room. "You guys can beat it. Assaulters, stick around. We got some family business to take care of."

We all waited as the admin folks made their way out of our Team room.

Sonny looked at us, "New guys, front and center. Congrats on making it to Blue Team. It's been an abbreviated work-up for you guys, but expectations are high. Gold Dust, you good?"

Gold Dust walked up to me and said "Sheff, here's your Bones patch. Congratulations, bro."

He placed in my hand a black square patch with a white skull and crossbones. Over the left eye of the skull was an eye-patch.

All the operators standing around us made their way over and shook our hands.

"Probation's over, boys," Gold Dust said. "You've earned a place here. Now you gotta keep it."

We loaded buses and headed out to the tarmac. We arrived ten minutes later, just as the last ISU (Individual Storage Unit) was getting loaded on our C-17. There were two C-17s sitting there, ramps open. One was going to Iraq and the other was ours, going back to Afghanistan. We said goodbye and hugged the other half of Blue Team as they boarded up the plane for Iraq. I grabbed an empty seat and clipped in my pack. I wondered to myself what would happen over the next few months.

The medic came around and gave each of us our pill packs in case we got shot and gave us our Ambien so we could rack out for the next sixteen hours. Shortly after take-off, we ascended the ISUs lining the center of the cargo bay in the belly of the plane and set up our little personal sleeping areas. Think REI-inspired gypsy camp. Three in-flight refuels later, the crew chiefs came over the loud speaker.

"Can I get everyone to start waking up and taking seats? We will be doing a combat landing in Bagram in thirty minutes."

I woke out of my stupor and we all climbed down and rolled up our bedrolls. It was always nice when the flight crew was cool and let us sleep up on top of the ISUs.

"RAMP!" We heard this yelled over all the noise of the four engines slowing down. The ramp cracked and my eyes watered from the hot-ass air and smell of jet fuel that poured into the cargo hold. I could see the lights of the military city in Afghanistan known as Bagram Air Field. It's a massive spectacle of military presence. There were dozens of buildings, networks of trailers, construction everywhere, as well as tanks, planes, hummers, and the like that crisscrossed the whole installation.

We grabbed our day packs and de-planed as the Sea Bees went to work on getting our ISUs loaded up on the flat beds and taken to Alpha Compound. As we headed to the bus, we walked behind a C-130 that was loading a bunch of Army grunts with their whole lives packed in massive backpacks. They lined up behind the plane and began to board. I only assumed they were on their way back home because the aircrew ground guide was using his red glowing batons to count heads as service members boarded. He was stopping at every female and proclaiming loudly as he waved the baton over their heads, "POOF, you're ugly again." "POOF, you're ugly again." "POOF, you're ugly again."

A few of us couldn't help but laugh our asses off as he said it to some female Army captain who was a bit over-sized and she commenced dressing him down.

We rolled into our area and immediately started turning over with the guys that were heading out. We had our own set-up separate from everyone else. Guys were sitting around getting suntans. They weren't doing anything. They were eating in the chow hall, working out in the gym, and having a scientific experiment to see who could sleep the longest.

We met the guys in the chow hall. They were all sitting over at a table by themselves. They all were in some combination of t-shirts and op cammie pants. Everyone else in the chow hall was dressed in perfect uniforms. I saw Jimmy and right away it started, “You guys ain’t doin’ shit, bro. We’ve been working in the chow hall.”

These guys looked bored as hell. Apparently, Al-Qaida had fled to Pakistan and, seeing that we were the main effort on the hook for Osama bin Shithead, we were about to be sitting on our thumbs, too.

I left the chow hall and walked over to the fire pit to talk to a few of the guys and find out what they’d done so far.

“Iraq is where it’s hot and heavy, bro,” one guy said.

“I’m finally here and it’s over? I feel like an asshole,” I grumbled to myself.

We finished turn over and got to work right away doing some low-vis snatch-and-grab work with the locals. Me and the boys would roll into a village with a couple of booger eaters and a picture of some Muslim terrorist, and we’d literally start clearing until we found him or had nothing else to clear. It was crazy. I’d have the entire village lined up and some source with us from God knows where would come by and identify if the guy was there or not. It was brutal.

“Where are the bad guys?” we’d ask.

Or we’d go set up a vehicle checkpoint from some vehicle description, whatever it was, a white Corolla usually. We’d literally stop every single white Corolla that came through.

It wasn’t all bad. I got to see some amazing scenery driving in Toyota pickups from Bagram to Kabul and then on to Jalalabad. I remember coming down out of the mountains into the JBAD Bowl. It was green fields next to a river and there were palm trees everywhere. It looked like what I thought Eden must be like.

It would be about five of us with fifty of the Afghans. Other than stopping every so often for prayer time, it was some uneventful operating.

Most of this type of work we did was with the Agency. Ground branch guys were always good dudes but, in my opinion, most of the standard CIA farm dipshit case officers sucked ass and had no business in a war zone. These tools were all politicians and had seen one too many movies.

It was going pretty routine. We'd wake up in the evening, eat, check if anything was going on, which it never was, and then go work out. Some nights I'd take a dirt bike up to the top of the ridgeline and watch the sun come up. It was always an amazing sight over the mountains. As beautiful as the scenery was, all I wanted was combat.

About three weeks had passed and we were spread out all over Afghanistan in small groups. Then we got a call. It was Sonny.

"Hey, Sheff, Westmore says we ain't waiting on Al Qaeda anymore. They might come back; they might not. Who gives a shit? There's plenty of bad guys here; let's go hunt Taliban. You guys pack it up and get back here to BAF…tonight. We got something real."

"Roger that, 2-2. We will be en route directly," I replied.

As we rolled back into Bagram, there were already guys in the ready room prepping gear, weapons, and ammo. Westmore came over to talk to us there, which was odd. He was the acting commanding officer in OEF. We all loved him. We never really saw the other guy. In combat, I mean.

"All right, fellas, listen up. This is no shit. The Army is asking for some help down south in Helmand. They are taking heavies and so are the local civilians. I'm clearing you guys hot to start hunting Taliban. Any questions? No? Good. Happy hunting, and you better damned well know I've got your backs from here. You need assets, let me know. See you guys soon."

I couldn't believe my ears. We had just been ordered to hunt Taliban and I should say that single order changed the course of the command's history forever. I called Shane who was already down south.

"Hey bro, what do you guys got down there?"

Shane said, "Bro, if y'all come down here right now, I swear to God, we'll kill people tonight."

Perfect, I thought to myself.

"Bro, we are en route to Kandahar tonight on a Talon. Come get us. It's game on!"

Then Eric, who chose like several others to be a vagina and not go with the twelve of us, starts in, "Oh, you guys aren't gonna do shit. Run around after wood smugglers and apple farmers down there. I'm going to stay here and bang that CIA chick I met in the gym a couple more times before deployment's over, get mortared, you know, whatever."

One of the guys slammed his mag in his rifle and sent the bolt home as he looked at Eric and shook his head.

"Cool, man, yeah, you go be all you can be or whatever."

We arrived down south at a place called Gecko. It was Mullah Omar's old compound. It was about one-hundred-twenty degrees in the daytime and this was the only place I'd ever seen in Afghanistan with a big-ass swimming pool. It made for a good place to lay up for a bit.

We rolled through a series of sand bags and gates in our Toyotas and got waved up to a massive compound gate that rolled away to the right. Johnny was standing there in board shorts and flip-flops to meet us. He waved us in and we all parked and dropped our kit.

"Hey, guys, happy to have you. We got these hooches set up for you. That's where you can put your gear while you're here. Pick a room, drop your shit, and meet in the SPA for the word."

The Strike Force Planning (SPA) area is where we did all our mission briefing.

I dropped my bag in an open room and pulled my Bible out. I set it on the small table next to the bed and stared at it for a minute. It gave me comfort.

When it was time to go, long after the sun had set, we met in the Ready Room to put on our gear. There were thirteen of us: eight SEALs, one CCT (Combat Control Team), one Air Force PJ (Para Jumper), one EOD (Explosive Ordnance Disposal Technician), and two seasoned Army Rangers.

Backup was being provided by the Quick Reaction Force (QRF), which was waiting for us on the runway next to a pair of CH-47 Chinooks—twin-engine, heavy-lift helicopters. We would always have a QRF, if possible, and most of the time it was comprised of Army Rangers.

As I finished gearing up, I realized nobody was talking. The room was alive with the sounds of buckles and zippers and the clank of weapons and assorted gear, and every last man was alone with his thoughts. I didn't know what they were thinking, but I was thinking that only about a third of these guys had seen real combat before and I wasn't in that third. People kept telling us we were the greatest soldiers on the planet, and maybe we had come to believe it a little—and, after all these years, we were getting ready to find out.

I was designated breacher for this mission, meaning I'd bring enough explosives to get us into just about anything. Even though I was a sniper when I was at SEAL Team Eight, I still had to prove myself worthy to be a sniper at Blue Team. The Recce Team, as they were known, was invite only at MOB VI.

I pulled my tan top on with "O POS NKDA" written with a Sharpie on my shoulder pockets (O Positive, No Known Drug Allergies). I had a tan plate carrier with chicken plates (body armor) in the front pockets. My H-gear shoulder harness held my water, ammo, grenades, med kit, morphine, pill pack, map, compass, GPS, knife, GU energy packets, radio and strobe. My secondary weapon, a Sig Sauer 239, was stowed in a holster on my hip. It had an extended magazine with a total of eleven 9mm rounds, one already locked and loaded. My primary weapon was a tried-and-true Colt M4 carbine with a 14-inch barrel, an ACOG 4 X 32 (advanced combat optical gunsight a power scope, with a suppressor that muted both the sounds and the muzzle flashes. The Colt also had a PEQ 2 laser sight on the front rail for infrared targeting. I slung it over my neck and, under my left arm, I stashed five extra magazines in my ammo belt, next to my breaching charge, a seven-foot C6 strip primed at both ends. My night vision goggles were strap-mounted to my Kevlar half-shell helmet. As I finished my gear prep and made my comms checks, it started to settle in that no one was coming around to check us. It was on each man individually to show up on time with the right gear every time. I glanced at my G-Shock. The next hard time was 2100 local. I had about ten minutes before I had to be in my seat in the SPA for the OPORD (Operational Order). I still remember walking into the SPA for that very first OPORD. There was a buzz of excitement because this was what we all wanted. I looked up at the wall covered in LCD screens. Each one had a different ISR feed. We had enough aerial reconnaissance assets to cover multiple targets through our entire area of operation, or AO.

I quietly found a seat and put in a dip. I remember thinking, Who are all these people?

We had all sorts of enablers, strap hangers and looky-loos. Everybody wanted to see the show. There was a real feeling that things were about to change.

"Good evening, fellas. I'm Sonny, Blue Team Troop Chief, for those of you who don't know. My callsign is 2-2. Target tonight is Mullah Da Dullah Lang. He is currently the Taliban's leader in Helmand."

I could see this dirt bag's picture on a kill/capture card that was on one of the screens. One of the large monitors had an overhead imagery and map overlay.

"I'll turn it over to Gold Dust for infil."

Gold Dust walked up to brief for Recce. "Hey, guys I'm Gold Dust, callsign India-1. I'm the Recce Team leader. It's gonna be a nine-klick walk tonight. Eight check points followed by ORP. Plan on about two hours of movement. Once we're on target, Recce Team will be here, here, and here." He pointed to the LCD screen with the Grid Reference Guide (GRG) macro. The GRG was a satellite overhead image that was gridded out so everyone could talk off the same map. It looked like an overhead of a large compound with an open courtyard and some building off to the side, but still contained within the compound.

Sonny took back over. "We've never been into this area before, so identify the target before you pull the trigger. Listen to your Team leaders. If we get hit on the way to the target, we will finish the fight and re-assess. HLZ is to the south, here…"

Sonny indicated the areas on the GRG.

"Johnny…"

"Okay, guys, I'm Johnny, Golf Team Leader, callsign Golf-1. Golf has main breach tonight. Sheff's got the strip charge for the gate and multiple door poppers. Please refer to MICRO GRG. We will be making entry on the east side and commence clearance this way. Special equipment, Sheff's got the ladder as well."

I took it in good humor. I was the new guy still.

Johnny looked over at Sonny, "Pending any question, back to you."

Sonny paused for a second and then said, "Ground Force Commander has final thoughts."

The GFC moved to the front of the room and looked at us. "Hey, fellas, all CAS calls go through me and I'll be co-located with Uniform-1. My callsign is 2-1. I'm clearing hot-to-drop bombs. If anyone has any questions, now's the time to ask."

We all had our game faces on. Nobody said anything.

"All right, guys, check the boards for Chalk loads and meet out at the birds."

I heard the 47s and felt the ground shaking as we got closer. I turned on my NVGs and could see the blades churning in the air. They glowed bright green as they sparked and ripped through the massive dust clouds. We jumped out of the trucks with all our gear on and did a quick check. Everyone was press-checking, taking a piss, and checking lasers. As I looked up at the two Chinooks, callsign Thunder 91 and Thunder 92, I knew I was on Chalk One and saw Johnny standing at the ramp, waiting to get a head count. Each bird carried two pilots, two front-door gunners with mini-guns, and two rear-door gunners with M60 machine guns.

There was a distinct high-pitched buzzing noise as I boarded the aircraft. I felt like I was walking through a massive hot air dryer. I hated flying. We boarded the helos, seven apiece, gave a "Full Head Count" call to the pilots and lifted off in unison.

Chapter 7
FIRST BLOOD

We sat cross-legged on the hard steel floor and clipped our lanyards into the metal D-rings. Even at that height and speed, thc desert heat made it feel like we were flying into a blow dryer. I was sweating like crazy, but the hot wind vacuumed the drops right off my temples. Some fifty minutes into the flight and right after I had filled my piss bottle, the radio squawked. My earpiece cracked as a voice came over comms, "2 Troop, this is 2-2, we're 10 minutes out. 10 minutes. ISR passes seven movers on target. OVER."

I launched my piss bottle out the back and each of us repeated the call down the line, hollering to make himself heard above the roar. Ten minutes! 10 minutes! 10 minutes!

Seven movers, I thought to myself. That meant seven fighting-age males moving around the compound. I could hardly wait. The anticipation was excruciating. I peered down the inside of the helo and saw Sonny up there. He held three fingers up.

"3 minutes, 3 minutes, 3 minutes."

NVGs were down and guys were ready.

"1 minute, 1 minute, 1 minute."

Through my leather gloves, I felt for the safety switch on my M4 with my thumb.

At this point, everyone was on a knee, and snipers were standing on the ramp holding on. The bird landed with a jolt and we unclipped and hauled ass.

We filed off and set a perimeter, picking up security positions and filling in the gaps. We fanned out three-hundred-sixty degrees. We waited in a tornado of dirt until the helos lifted off. The crew chief gave a thumbs up and then disappeared in the brown-out.

Then it got real quiet, almost eerie. We took off in patrol formation and began a long-ass hump to the target. I was a new guy again—breacher—carry the ladder, carry whatever. I was uncomfortable, I didn't feel good, I didn't know where exactly, geographically, we were going.

The snipers led the way. Dead of night, one hundred degrees in the desert, and I could already feel the sweat soaking through my clothes. Chafed nuts and swamp ass up and coming.

I'm watching assholes; nobody's left the compound, right? We know these guys might be around. Maybe one guy leaves; okay, we watched him come out, he's out by the river, and he's coming back. He took a shit. So they're watching this. If anybody leaves, they let us know.

Over the eight-kilometer route, we crawled through mud flats and crept through dry riverbeds and ravines and stunted brush, trying not to sound like a herd of buffalo. I couldn't seem to get the sand and grit out of my mouth. And I couldn't stop thinking about what lay ahead. My job initially would be to find the main entry gate and load it up with an explosive charge. If anything was locked or closed, I was going to blow that, too. Then I'd get to be number one man through the doorway. But I had no idea what to expect. All I knew was that, at some point, we would reach the target compound, and that it was my responsibility to get us in.

Maybe I'll see some actual bad guys for once, I thought to myself.

I prayed. "Dear Heavenly Father, I love you and I thank you for everything you've given me. I ask for protection for all of us. I ask for your angels to be here tonight. I can't do this without you, Lord, and I thank you for being present. Amen."

I looked up at Johnny in front of me and his ass was wet with sweat. It was disgusting. Summer nights in southern Afghanistan suck. I saw past him, up to where Gold Dust and the other snipers were. The snipers always knew everything that was going on. They'd be up planning, working with pilots, and looking at routes while most dudes slept in and only woke up for the OPORD. I wanted to go to Recce bad. I wanted to be up front, leading.

The moon was out, extremely bright, and I looked under my NVGs and saw my shadow on the ground. I was like, man, this is not good. It's bright as shit.

About four kilometers into the patrol, I started noticing compounds. We navigated around and over what seemed like a maze of compound walls for several hundred meters. All quiet on the Helmand front as we moved closer to the target compound.

The point man came over comms. "Two Troop, this is India One. I passed check point one, OVER."

I glanced down at the GPS on my wrist. Of the eight checkpoints, we were down to one. One kilometer to go, as the crow flies, that is.

Soon after, we reached a dry riverbed about two hundred meters wide and slowed to a crawl. Everybody peered through their NVGs and took a good long look around, scanning the surrounding terrain. No movement, nothing. We crossed very slowly and in pairs. We were still a kilometer away from the target compound, but the concern was knowing we could very well have been watched. We kept creeping, trying to avoid stepping on the dry, crunchy leaves.

Finally, the big mud walls surrounding the target compound came into view. It was about two hundred meters away. We stopped. All of us were drenched in sweat. Through my NVGs, I saw a wall running along the east side, flanked by a massive trench. The trench was about five feet deep and seemed to run all the way to the compound. On the far side of the trench, I saw a poppy field stretching as far as the eye could see. As I took a knee, put my Camelbak hose into my mouth and drew a long pull. Nothing like a mouth full of hot water when you're thirsty.

Another hundred yards and we'd be at our Operational Ready Point (ORP), where we'd take cover to prep breaching charges and ladders or special equipment. We'd usually get one more intel update before moving forward to assault. I remember noticing weird mounds of rocks everywhere with little flags on them. We were in a graveyard. The savages don't bury their bodies, like we do; they wrap them in sheets, lay them on the ground and cover them with rocks. I then took notice that we were hanging out like a pair of gigantic balls on a tiny dog.

Right then, the point man gave a hold signal. The patrol stopped.

Gold Dust came over comms, "Two Troop, India-1. Recce has eyes on one mover. Appears to be armed. Stand fast."

I saw his IR laser illuminate the hilltop to my left about a hundred meters away.

Holy shit! There's a guy right there! What are we waiting for?

I spat a string of Copenhagen and looked up at the point man, still as a statue and, when I turned back, my vision panning, I froze. I thought I'd seen something; I *knew* I'd seen something. I reached up to my eyes for NVGs and adjusted the dial for clarity. The silhouette of a man came into view, a lone sentry. He was on his knees, on the hill above, his head cocked at an odd angle, as if he'd heard something. He was very still, actively listening.

I looked toward the point man again. He was looking at the same sentry and must have been thinking what I was thinking—Maybe he heard us, maybe not—and a moment later he signaled for us to keep moving. We pressed on, trying to keep quiet.

We were all now watching this guy. He obviously heard us or something. I saw him perk up. He was looking around and hadn't looked back in our direction yet.

I turned to look at the compound again and reached for my breaching charge. It was powerful enough to blast through mud, concrete, steel or whatever else these guys had waiting for us. I rested the charge on my left shoulder and could feel the edge of my explosive strip charge with its plastic hydrogel cover digging into the side of my neck. I didn't want to touch it. I could feel the sweat running from the top of my head down my face to rest on my upper lip. I watch the sentry turn and look at us. There's no way he doesn't see us, I thought to myself.

We kept moving and, a few seconds later, the sentry jerked himself up to his feet. Now I *knew* the guy had heard us. He was looking in our direction. The moon was behind us, suddenly brighter, and I could pretty much imagine what he was seeing: fourteen silhouettes moving toward the compound.

I felt cortisol dump into my guts, responding to the stress, with a follow-up shot of adrenaline close behind. The hairs stood up on the back of my neck. Then I noticed that the sentry had something in his hand—a radio, maybe?—and I released the safety on my M4 as I raised it to my shoulder and activated the infra-red laser. We were all watching this one guy, waiting, wondering. Suddenly, he turned and all these heads started popping up. Here we go. There's a ton of guys up there!

Our Afghan/American interpreter started picking up chatter on his I-COMM radio, which was a radio the enemy used. We always carried one to listen to enemy communications. He looked like he was about to shit his pants; there must have been ten fighters up there. Guys are getting belt-fed machine guns and turning them toward us. It was about to get sporty. I dumped my breaching charge.

"Get in the ditch," Johnny yelled.

I spit my dip wad out and Shane yelled at me, "Hey, bro, they got guns and they're maneuvering."

Our senses had gone through the roof. I felt like I saw, hear and smell everything. All of a sudden, it was like I was floating. I could feel every grain of sand under my boot and smell the gun oil in my M4. Things seemed to slow down and get very easy to process.

Shane opened up with his Squad Automatic Weapon (SAW) and the damned thing jammed on him right away.

Here's what I'll tell you: When I looked at that guy and I watched him take aim with his belt-fed PKM, I was like I know I can shoot him but I've never done this before. Like, I'm pretty sure I can shoot. I guess I'm going to shoot this guy. I'm going to shoot him now.

You have this little dialogue with yourself. Very quickly. But it's a bit unnatural.

As soon as I landed in the ditch, my gun was up, my finger on the trigger. Before I fired a single shot, the air around me was already crackling with bullets. I still remember every detail. The guy had a long beard, and he was emptying his PKM in our direction, his whole body shaking. I put the laser on his chest and squeezed the trigger. I watched him drop to his knees for a moment until the force of the following two rounds sent him tumbling backward out of sight. For a split second, I actually acknowledged to myself that I had just killed a man.

More targets popped up and fought or ran. We kept shooting, even as the bullets whizzed past, and I felt as if I couldn't miss. Everything seemed to be happening in slow motion. The night was crackling with gunfire, but it sounded somehow distant and muted, and I felt like I had all the time in the world. I would paint the next man's chest with my laser, squeeze the trigger, and the son of a bitch would drop. I'd paint the next man's face and squeeze and his head would come apart and he'd drop. And we just kept going, dumping rounds, taking out one man after another. And they kept coming.

Everything was so sharp: The smells, the taste of salt in my mouth, the way the bodies fell. The enemy fighters were moving in what seemed like slow motion. One by one we cut these guys in half, but it was far from over.

We were engaged on all sides and bullets and rockets were coming from every direction, it seemed. Tracer fire lit up the sky.

"CONTACT LEFT!"

I pivoted and dropped a fighter hitting us with AK fire from a poppy field.

Gold DUST came over the radio. "2-Troop, this is Juliet-1. We got multiple Military Aged Males (MAMs) massing at this time, starting to maneuver."

Gold Dust and the snipers had moved up to high ground and were peering through their rifle optics and thermal scopes. From their position, they saw multiple MAMs trying to outflank us.

Uniform-1 and the GFC made it up to where we were now and I could hear Uniform-1 on the radio.

"Hog 1-1, this is Uniform-1, Troops in Contact, requesting danger close fire mission, OVER…"

"Uniform-1, Hog-1…Roger, copy Troops in Contact."

"Hog-1, Uniform-1 is marked by strobe and sparkling target at this time, OVER."

"Roger that, Uniform -1, you boys get your heads down."

Me and Shane hustled over to a small hill and saw fighters approaching.

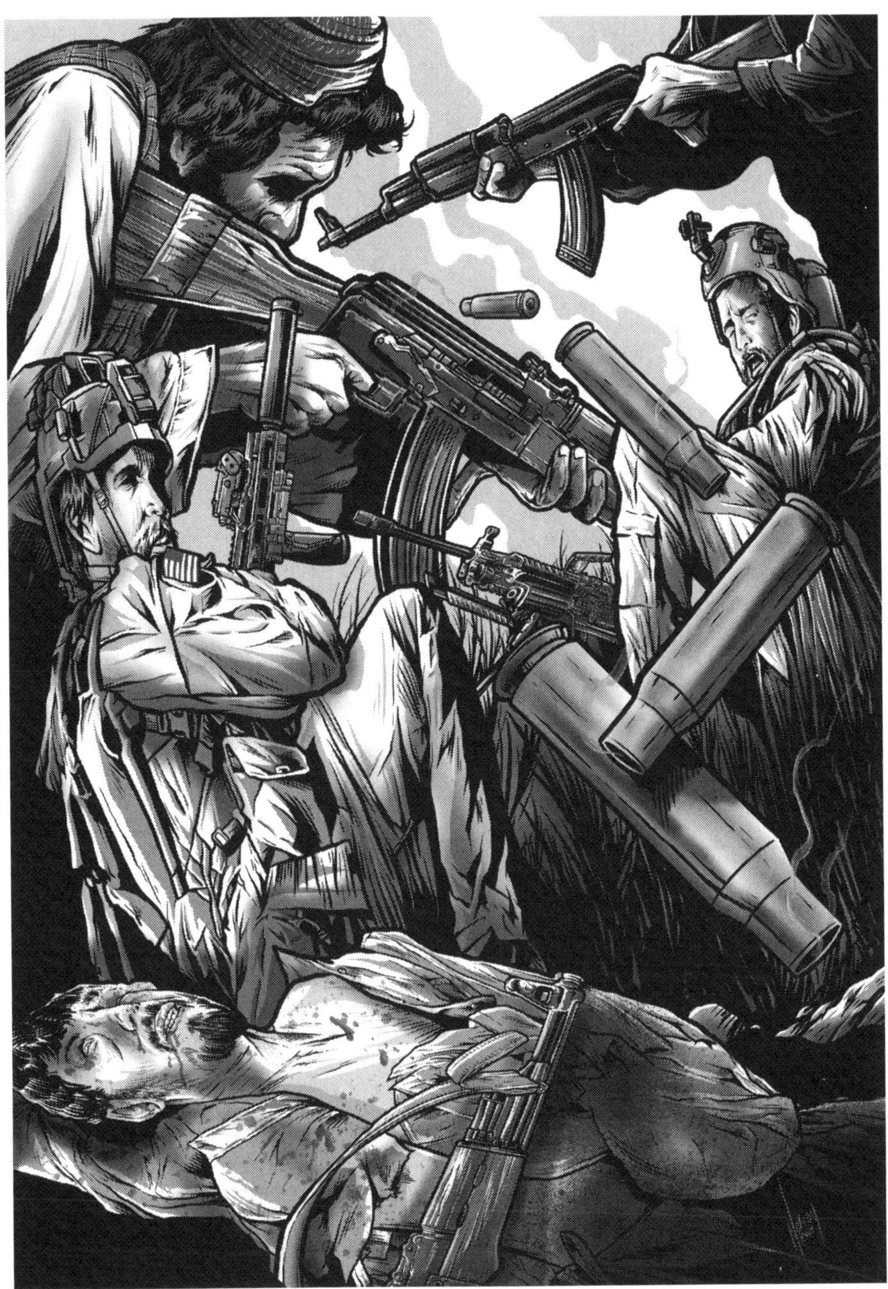

Then we heard a sound like the sky tearing open. We looked up. An A-10 Warthog carved a sharp turn and leveled off with its rotary cannons unleashing. It laid into the enemy mass with a deafening

BBBBRRRRRRRRRRRRRRRRP as body and building parts went everywhere. It was awesome.

Shane finally had his SAW back up and running full auto.

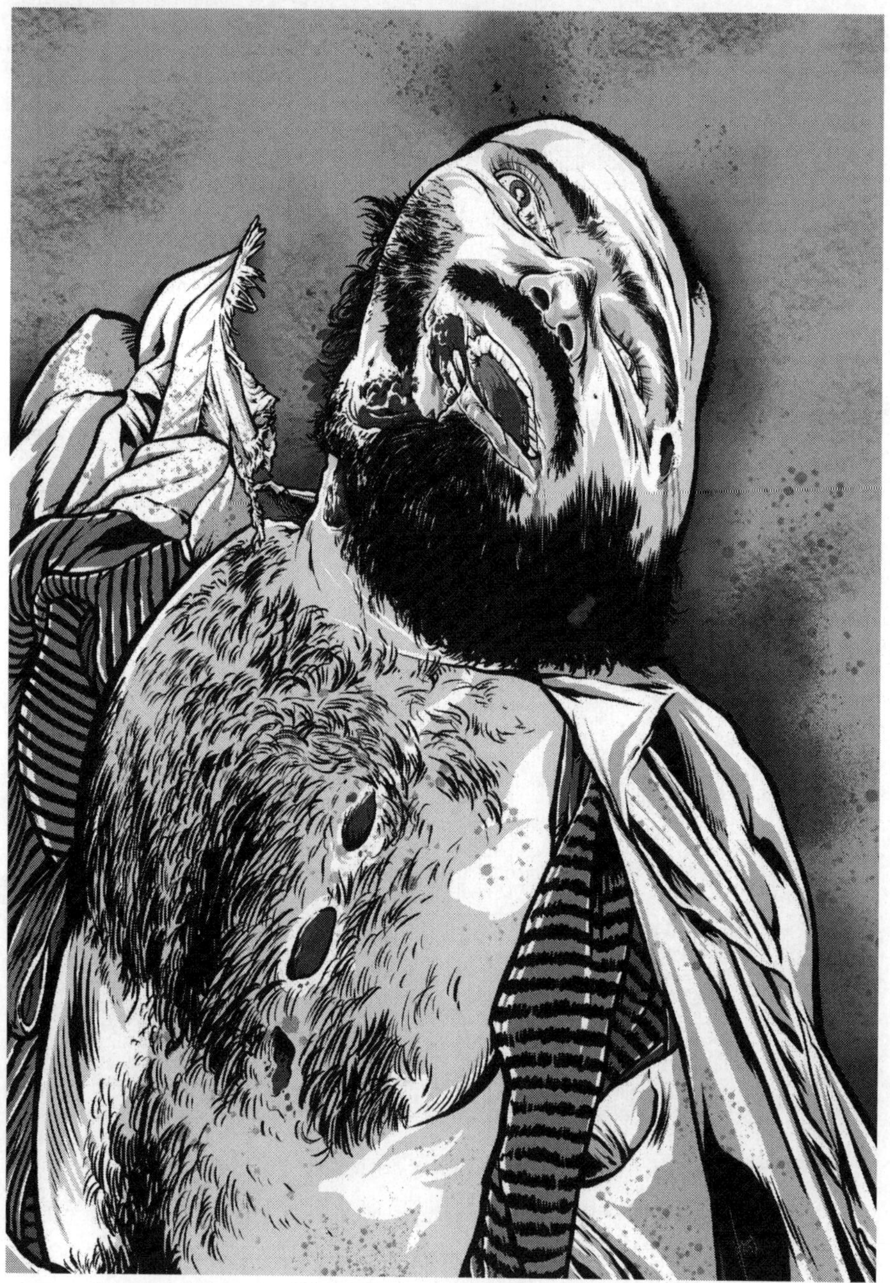

"COCKSUCKER!" Johnny yelled from the right flank. "It's okay, man, I literally killed everyone."

The fire-fight lasted almost four hours with multiple waves of fighters coming to us. It was getting light out. Dawn was less than an hour away.

The shooting had died down enough for us to notice the quiet. I checked my ammo and it was low.

Luckily, our terp was petrified scared and in the fetal position still, so I grabbed all his extra ammo. Then I walked over and looked at a couple of the bodies just lying there lifeless. I stared at the bullet holes in the first guy that I killed. It's an unnerving thing. It felt unreal. I just wanted to take in the reality of it all for a moment.

We didn't make it to the actual compound we were targeting until late that next morning. The sun was up now and the enemy was keeping its distance, for a while anyway. We made the decision to continue to the target compound. Almost immediately we began taking fire again.

Close Air Support (CAS) had already been approved by Westmore and fast movers were inbound. They came in, guns and bombs blazing and literally leveled the uncleared compounds ahead of us. We moved up through the rubble and cleared what was left.

We saw across the riverbed, about seven hundred meters out, there appeared to be hundreds of people massing. We got updates from ISR that the groups appeared to be massing and moving toward us. We immediately called for EXFIL and began to make a hasty withdrawal.

The rangers had set up several blocking positions to the south, affording us safe movement to the Helo Landing Zone (HLZ). The birds came in covered by A-10s, and slammed into the makeshift landing zone. I ran onto the CH-47 and clipped in. I sat there, wondering if we'd make it out. It seemed like it took forever to get out of there but, once we made it up out of the brown-out dust storm and were out of small arms range, I sat back against the fuel tanks and closed my eyes.

I woke to a tap on the shoulder and, as my eyes focused, I saw a bearded face and felt my hand taken. I looked down at my hand and an Army Ranger had put a can of tobacco in it. I took a dip, and went to hand it back and he leaned next to my ear and yelled, "Keep it, bro."

We landed back at the firebase. It was hard to contain how excited we all were. We had enemy blood all over us. We had gunpowder and dirt in our mouth that crunched our teeth. Our bloodshot eyes were almost sealed closed from the amount of soot, sweat and dust caked under our eyelids. No one cared. We were all happy to have lived through that shit.

I remember thinking that all the nights I spent in BUD/S exhausted, wet and sandy were just the price of admission for this. As much as I wanted to take a hot shower and just go to bed, there was still post-op gear prep and refit that had to be done. This would become our life in the Teams. Warfare was our new routine.

I finished cleaning my guns from all the dust and carbon. I reloaded my mags and grenades because I'd gone through damn near everything. Seven magazines with twenty-eight rounds apiece, almost all expended on the enemy. I changed all my batteries out—NVGs, GPS, scope, laser. We rebuilt some more C6 strip charges and primed them at both ends with detonating cord.

When I finally had a moment to myself, I sat down on my bed and typed an email to Leslie and one to my parents. I told them I loved them and that it had been a "good one." I couldn't go into detail but they knew what it meant. I ended the emails asking for their continued prayers for my Team and me. It was comforting to feel this connection to my family for a brief moment of normalcy after experiencing something that changed me forever. After I hit "send," I sat there in the quiet and clenched my Bible. Guys got comfortable in flip-flops and board shorts and, once all the equipment was accounted for, we all cracked a beer.

"Where's the Ambien?"

Chapter 8
ROUND TWO

I sat down with a plate of food, closed my eyes, and said a prayer. I thanked God I was still breathing. Then I scarfed down some fake-ass eggs, thawed out burritos, and washed a hash brown and biscuit down almost whole with some milk that tasted like ass. I was way past eating for pleasure at this point and it had become more of just a survival decision.

We were all thinking the same way. We were all feeling something we had never felt before—about combat, about the enemy, about each other. I had never felt anything like it in my life and I loved it.

It's a hell of a thing taking other men's lives and listening to them die. I remembered not everyone died right away after being shot. I watched some coil up and begin to moan and make gurgling sounds as shock set in and their pulse increased before fading. Blood pressure weakens and drops.

I couldn't help but relive the whole night as I laid there and tried to sleep. I felt like I just closed my eyes for a second but I must have dosed off for a while. I opened my eyes in a slumber to this wiry, ripped-out tattooed maniac we called the Butcher. He was our EOD guy.

"Wakey, wakey, eggs and bakey. Hey, man, we've got something big going on in the JOC. Last night's target is crawling. You may want to come check this out."

I headed over to grab Shane. I stuck my head in his room and flicked on the light.

"Headed to the SPA, buddy. Something's up."

Guys were cramming into the SPA and around the ISR monitors showing the target area. People were everywhere. It looked like an anthill. The video on the screen was produced by a FLIR system on a drone. The images on screen are black and white.

Guys were muttering to each other.

"Wow, look at what we did."

"Yep, we definitely stirred this shit up now."

Obie was our intel guy. He was worth his weight in gold. He walked up to the front of the room and referred to the monitor.

"This is very abnormal. We've never seen anything like this. Hitman 73 is the Pred drone covering the target here. Hitman 74 is following this pack of enemy fighters."

I looked at what appeared to be several hundred Taliban fighters moving very quickly from village to village, gaining numbers as they went.

Johnny leaned over to me and said, "We're going kinetic when they stop to hunker down for the night. When they take over a little village somewhere in the next few hours, we'll drop on 'em when they lay up.

We watched Sonny talk into a speakerphone to Westmore, who was back in BAF running the show.

I could hear Westmore's voice over comms, "You guys are cleared hot for pre-assault fires."

Sonny stepped out of the side office. "Everyone get a good meal and drink plenty of water. You guys can clearly see what we're gonna be up against. We'll all meet back up in a half hour to start planning."

The plan was to INFIL with four CH-47s, two for our troop and two for the Rangers. The AC-130 and other supporting fixed wing assets were to drop bombs before we touched down on the ground. This was a special circumstance due to the overwhelming enemy force. All military-aged males were considered hostile.

The Rangers were going in with us to set blocking positions for squirter control. A squirter was any MAM who ran from the target during the assault.

We made our way back over to the JOC and Sonny got right to it. "We're gonna go straight to the Y tonight; we're not gonna to do a full offset."

That meant that we would be landing just outside of small arms range but close enough for everyone to know we're there. It gets a bit dicey. It's gonna be a big fires mission. Basically, hit it with the bombs from the aircraft, and we're going right in to SSE the bodies. Uniform1, you're up."

"Good evening. I'm Uniform-1. All CAS calls tonight will go through me. I will be running the stack tonight. Fires platforms will remain over target until EXFIL is complete. I will be monitoring Fires Net as well as Command Net. Pending questions, I turn it over to Papa-1."

"Okay, gents, Papa-1, in and out on Chalk 2. The medical plan is as follows: We will set up casualty collection here and here."

He pointed to screen with GRG on it. "In case of mass casualty, the CASEVAC and CSAR bird will be Thunder 91, staged at Salerno with SRT and the flight surgeon. Pending your questions, over to you, sir…"

That was the plan. And we were dismissed to jock up. We were all talking anxiously outside, having a smoke and getting our op-kit on when Johnny stuck his head outside and said, "Hey, get in here; it's about to go down."

We hurried inside the Joint Operations Center (JOC). It was the command center where the analysts and the head shed sat at rows of computers and monitored the operations. Uniform-1 was in front by the big screen.

"ROUNDS AWAY!"

We watched with bated breath as this long column of enemy fighters lay in stillness. The problem is, and this is a major problem, if they don't all die right away, then it falls on us to clean up any stragglers before they can escape the area. This was hinging on that.

"BOOM!"

They missed. A hellfire missile impacted the ground near the fighters and the detonation on the thermal image just showed a white screen in the JOC. After the image came back, we saw squirters running everywhere. They were running in and around a maze of compounds.

I looked at Shane, "They missed! Holy shit, bro, they missed."

Shane, shook his head, "Well, there's no fucking way…there's no way we're still going into that now, right?"

"We'd be flying into a pretty horrible situation now," I said.

Sonny stepped up, "Fellas, relax, they're gonna keep hitting them while we fly in."

My heart was in my stomach. I was thinking to myself, this is how it is? Is this how it's gonna be every time?

Guys were making final gear checks and preps and I sat down on my pelican case and pulled my Bible out.

"Let's go!" Sonny yelled as he walked out of the room. "The birds are spinning; get out there. We're going."

I quietly read to myself before I stepped outside. *Thou shalt not be afraid for the terror by night; nor for the arrow that flieth by day. A thousand shall fall at thy side, and ten thousand at thy right hand, but it shall not come nigh thee. Only with thine eyes shalt though behold and see the reward of the wicked.*

We all jumped into the back of Toyota pickups from the compound to ride out to the 47s. I saw our pair sitting there spinning, and further down the flight line the Rangers were piling off buses onto the other helos.

The image was still in my head of the ISR feed; hundreds of fighters stirred up now. I knew that's what we were flying into. And, as we lifted off, I already couldn't wait for the thirty-second call so we could just get outta this cocksucker and fight for ourselves.

"3 minutes! 3 minutes! 3 minutes!" my earpiece squawked.

We were all up on one knee, trying to see out the gunners' windows.

We saw the buildings blowing up as we came in…boom! boom!

Shane yelled, "RPG! RPG!" as he peered out the left-door gunner window.

They were firing everything they had at us. I didn't see those, thank God. We came in hot and slammed so hard it put all of us in a pile in the middle of the floor. We all scrambled to our feet and hauled ass… straight into explosions all around us. It was chaos for a moment. Both of our fire Teams went straight into leapfrogs, guns to bear, movements like football plays. Johnny's Team moved up first and laid down suppressive fire. Then Gold Dust's Team moved up and suppressed for Johnny. Rounds were snapping all over the place. It went on like this until we could gain a little foothold and hold some ground. There was a brief lull in the fight as the enemy tried to anticipate our next moves and out-maneuver us.

I saw a massive compound right in front of me maybe eighty yards and could see an alleyway beside it with trees and a canal full of water. There was a lot of movement down there. Back up on the second floor of the building, heads started popping up. I began engaging and all hell broke loose again. We got hit from the front and the right flank. Leapfrogging back, I put my laser on a guy and dumped him. Another one got right in the window where the last guy was and I sent two into his chest. To my right, I could see Shane dump three dudes in rapid succession, blasting them all into the canal. One tried to climb out and I face-shot him right back in.

Guys with 203s were now launching Golden Eggs into the windows and doing a number on this one compound full of bad guys. It was like shooting fish in a barrel. There were bodies everywhere. As they started to pile up. I wondered how many people I killed. But more than anyone else.

Rounds snapped overhead

Uniform-1 was literally the only guy standing up and he was now walking backward through the chaos, seemingly oblivious, like a guy searching for a cell phone signal.

"2-Troop, this is Uniform-1. We're gonna start calling CAS immediately. We need to push back to the south another hundred meters. We got Slasher on station!"

The Spectre gunship AC-130, callsign Slasher, had put himself into a tight orbit over the target area and these guys made music!

"Slasher 1-1, this is Uniform-1 marked by strobe. Lasing target at this time, OVER."

Uniform-1 painted an infrared figure eight on the side of the compound we needed gone and the aircraft matched sparkle.

"2-Troop, this is Uniform-1...Rounds away, get down. Danger close!"

The ground started shaking as we all sucked mud and dropped to our chests.

1-0-5 rounds and forty mike-mike grenades came raining down like a firestorm from God.

We continued to push forward after a few gun runs and it got very quiet. There were bodies hanging in trees, and we had to walk over piles of dead or dying Taliban fighters. Dudes were blown inside out and splayed open like some kind of zombie movie.

Over the next four hours, we commenced to methodically clearing, compound to compound and room to room. I went through four frag grenades attempting to kill barricaded enemy shooters. Then I dropped a small building with an over-pressure grenade and expended most of my ammo. I was even taking my breaching charges and clacking off the four-second delays before throwing them in the rooms for some kind of shock to the enemy before we entered.

I paired up with Johnny and we made our way up to the doorway of another compound. It had a blanket draped across the doorway. Without a word we split the doorway, me on one side, Johnny on the other. Johnny grabbed the blanket and started to slowly pull it back for me. Something hit the blanket and I heard Tink…Tink…Tink…

"GRENADE!" I yelled.

It blew as we both dove for the ground. Johnny got it in both legs and I took a tiny piece in the hand. I looked over at him. He was clearly in pain and rolling in front of the doorway. I grabbed the shoulder strap of his H-gear and dragged his ass out of the way. Shane and Gold Dust were sprinting to back us up and, without hesitation, jumped over us and into the room, dumping full belt-fed auto as they cleared. There were four fighters hunkered down in there. They all got hosed.

I threw Johnny's arm over my shoulder and we ditty-mowed back to some cover. He was bleeding through his pants.

"Papa-1, this is Golf-6…move to my strobe at this time…OVER."

The PJ got to me and started working on Johnny's legs. He could see we were stressed about Johnny's wounds, but he stayed super-calm.

He started working and said, "I got him, Sheff. He's gonna be fine. Johnny, you're gonna be fine, brother."

I looked back up to where Shane was. They dropped the building with a thermo. It was a good one. Then my earpiece cracked...

"2-Troop, this is 2-2. Hold what you got. Start wrapping it up and get the prisoners and get prepped for EXFIL. Immediately...Uniform-1... Call it in."

"2-2...Uniform-1...Roger, birds are 10 mikes out.... OVER."

"2-Troop, this is Juliet-1...Recce is taking it out. Moving to HLZ Black."

I looked at the PJ. "Papa-1, we gotta move. Johnny, you good to walk, brother?"

"Yeah, should be. You might have to give me a hand."

Johnny couldn't walk. I threw his ass up on my shoulder and just kind of jogged through the carcasses. I laid him up against this big-ass tree next to the canal, behind cover. I remember I could actually hear guys dying around us still. It was like what I imagined Hell must sound like. Weeping and gnashing of teeth, sayeth the text. I had a little red headlamp around my neck and I fired it up and went to work with the PJ, reassessing and making sure none of Johnny's dressings had come loose.

The Butcher came up and held security for us. While we were doing that, automatic gunfire erupted all over the place. We were engaged again and shooting down basically every alleyway and any rooftop where we could see movers. They were all over, still coming out and taking pot shots and we were trying to hold them back.

Sonny came over comms. "Two Troop, 2-2, search as many bodies as you can and get photos if you can."

They wanted photos of everybody, if it was safe. So we started pulling guys out of the canal and turning them over. I would take a piece of one-inch, tie it around their wrist and pull their bodies back out. The Butcher would hold his gun on them, give them a couple security rounds if they were still alive. Take a picture, move on.

We left at least one hundred bodies back there. I remember thinking at the time, how far are we going to take this? We couldn't just keep hitting and hitting. We were running out of night. When we finally got on the birds, I remember yelling. I was overjoyed to be alive in the air, high and dry, away from that hell down there. I remember sitting on one of the prisoners. Because we throw these guys on board, they have a mask on. They can't see shit anyway; they just pile up on the floor. I was sitting on one of them to keep him down, then closed my eyes for a minute and thanked God for another victory.

The rest of that ride back was a blur…almost surreal. I mostly stared out into the morning, dozing a little in the crisp mountain air.

We flew to the outstation. We landed and Johnny was off to the hospital. It was actually a Canadian hospital out there. I dropped my gear in the Ready Room and headed over looking for Johnny.

"What's up, bro. You good?"

"Yeah, man, all good. Couple stitches. Be on a cane for a minute but no worries."

I glanced over at a few of the Rangers that had been wounded also.

"How 'bout you, boys, y'all good, too? Good work last night, by the way."

"Yeah, it was. Thanks for checking on us."

I stood there for a bit and looked at all the wounded guys from various backgrounds and from different missions. It was kinda crazy how we were all there together fighting against this same evil. None of us wanted to die. But we believed in what we were doing so deeply that we were prepared to sacrifice our own lives in the service of our country.

As far as MOB VI, though, we'd been baptized. This wasn't indirect fire on base or an IED in a road somewhere. It wasn't just smoking some asshole while he lay sleeping in bed. It was close quarters combat. And we had survived. We'd won. And, more than anything, we had gone into the enemy's backyard, taking the fight to them.

Training didn't really emotionally prepare us for combat. Combat prepared us, it turned out. It made sense to me out there. Anybody can be a hero in training. Combat separates the warriors. Everything else went away and my mind was quiet.

After that op, all of us were on some kind of high. I flew on to Bagram with the prisoners and a few other guys in my Team and then jumped in the truck to head back to my outstation. It was about a three-hour drive to the outstation outside of Kabul, up in the mountains, and I couldn't wait to get off that base. What a circus.

We would be up operating and fighting for a full night, we'd get back with prisoners every morning, and we wouldn't be able to leave the base and go back to war because Disney would be—Disney was the name of the main road through Bagram Air Field (which we all thought was fitting)—and it would be shut down for all the Hooahs to have their morning power walk. So they'd be out there shuffling on the street, but we weren't allowed to drive on it. So we would have to wait on base for about two hours from whenever it was—5 a.m. to 7 a.m.—because there was no vehicle traffic allowed.

Of course, we did it anyway and got yelled at. Seatbelts. I've literally been pulled over on that base in Afghanistan because my vehicle didn't have seatbelts. What a douchebag that guy was. "Dude, what are you going to do, take my driving privileges away?"

The base cop faggots would be watching for us to drive by. "You don't have doors on your vehicle."

"Well, I'm driving a Humvee with no doors on it."

"Well, you need your seatbelt on and where's your helmet?"

You know what I mean? "It's in the back with night vision and the rest of my warfighting shit." We'd get pulled over just so they could look at us.

Once we cleared the gate and started the drive back out into the mountains, I actually remember feeling calm and happy. The trucks were outfitted Up-armored Toyota HiLux 4x4s. I had all my shit on. I had a LAW rocket (Light Anti-Tank Weapon) behind my seat. My passenger had a LAW rocket behind his seat, so they were just sitting ready. We were refitted with ammo, extra mags, frags, smokes, and food. We were warriors. And we finally had a war.

Chapter 9
WARPAINT

Coming home from that deployment felt good. I had legit war stories, the kind of engagements everyone wanted to live through and talk about. I wasn't home an hour and Shane was already sitting on his motorcycle in his garage pissing off the neighbors. Shane and I had bought houses next door to each other in a neighborhood with a bunch of other Team guys.

It made sense to us. Once we all knew we were gonna make it through Green Team and stay in the area, we figured why not get houses close so the families had each other to rely on. In theory, it was genius. In reality, it meant if anyone was going out, we were all going out. Leslie was thrilled about the arrangement.

I told Leslie goodbye and she gave me a look that wasn't hard to interpret. I fired up my Harley and me and Shane proceeded to set off a series of car alarms as we tore out of the neighborhood.

We rolled up on our Harleys outside a bar called Clutch. Most of us had bikes, all Harleys, usually straight pipes and ape hangers, and we took any excuse we could get while we were home to ride somewhere and have a beer together.

We pulled up with mufflers blasting and firing like a daisy chain of shot-gun blasts. Guys were standing around the porch and the parking lot smoking cigarettes and looking at bikes. Clutch was our local hang-out and it had flags and operator pictures all over the walls. It was just outside the gate, close to base, and usually our first stop back from deployment.

Shane and I walked in and saw guys at the long bar already ordering the first round. It was Johnny, Noah, Gold Dust, Medlow, and Eric the prick. Medlow and Eric were from another troop, cocky as the rest of us, but brothers just the same. Nonetheless, we got right into it without sparing anyone's emotions.

I took a shot of Jack, grabbed my Yuengling, and commenced to tell the tale.

"Well, no shit, I kicked the night off and face-shot the first guy at maybe eighty yards, while taking a full belt of ammo at the face like pulp fiction, bro…"

Shane gathered himself from almost choking and said, "Dude, shut the fuck up!"

"Ah," I said, "you're just mad because your gun jammed."

"Oh, you dick, you think you shot everyone."

"That's because I did," I said. "I literally shot everyone."

Johnny leaned in, "Yeah, maybe, but I killed them all."

Eric rolled his eyes and stated, "Shit, man, I can't believe we missed it."

Then Medlow offered, "I can't believe I wasn't there. We gotta listen to this!"

"Yeah, I'd be depressed, too, if I were you guys. Hey, I hear you knocked that chick up though."

"Classy," Shane said as he stole a cigarette from behind the bar.

"At least I got laid on deployment."

Then Johnny swills the rest of his Jack and says to Medlow, “Actually, bro, after this we’re all going to your mother’s house, so we’re good, too.”

Then my phone went off. It was my brother. He was getting some ink from Joey Nobody. Joey did all our Warpaint. He was the only guy most of us ever trusted to do any of our tattoos. We all had dozens of hours in the chair with Joey. He had tattooed Psalm 91 in Hebrew on my back, and covered both of my arms with sleeves. I probably had a total of about sixty hours in the chair with him. He wasn’t in the military, but he definitely served his country. Actually, he served as a kind of therapist for a lot of us. He came up slinging ink in New York and was elite in his own right.

“Hey, my brother’s getting his sleeve finished up. Let’s roll over to Joey’s.”

Shane and Noah bumped past me laughing.

“Race you there.”

I was on my old kick start, and Shane and Noah both fired their bikes up and peeled out.

“Later, asshole!”

They took off but I wasn’t far behind. I ended up racing through three red lights but I beat them to Joey’s. I always won all races, always.

Joey’s shop was badass. It was tucked away in this metal warehouse that served as a motorcycle shop for guys to work on their own bikes. We rolled up on our Harleys and parked outside the open roll-up door to the place. There were all kinds of rat-looking badass bikes up on jacks, or in various stages of completion. We walked passed a couple of dudes working on their bikes and I could see the plain door in the back that just said WARPAINT. I took note of a sign in the garage that I would later steal. It said, “If you think our prices are too high, bring your ol’ lady around and we’ll dicker.”

When I walked in, I saw my brother Brian in the chair getting worked on by Joey right beside him with his ink gun going. There was a Gold Team flag on the wall behind them and a large Bible was open to a picture of the crucifixion of Christ, illustrated by Gustav Dore. A lot of me and my brother's ink was inspired by this artist. The movie Platoon was playing on a flat screen on the wall.

"Hey, bro, that ink looks badass, Joey!"

Joey removed his glove and shook my hand.

"Thanks, bro, good to see you. We're on hour five right now so I could use a break."

Shane walked in and grabbed the Jack. "What's up, Brian? Sorry you didn't come to Blue with us, bro."

Brian held up an empty glass and jingled it. "All good. I heard deployment was a real bash, bro." He looked at Joey. "Smoke break?"

"You know it. My eyes are starting to water," Joey replied.

"Bum one, Joey?"

"Times two…Better yet, just grab the pack, Joey," Shane said as he grabbed the bottle.

I lagged back with my brother for a second. I gave him a hug; I hadn't seen him in quite a while. We were always together growing up in west Texas. He's been my best friend as long as I can remember, and we always looked out for each other. The last few years, though, we were on opposite schedules. He had come to SEAL Team Six but was not allowed to be on the same Team with me.

"I'm just glad you guys made it home," he said.

We walked outside and circled up. It was story time and it began again.

"Okay, let's hear this shit."

Shane took over immediately, "So, no shit, there we were, bro, coming in on final and I'm up on a knee already ready to fire…"

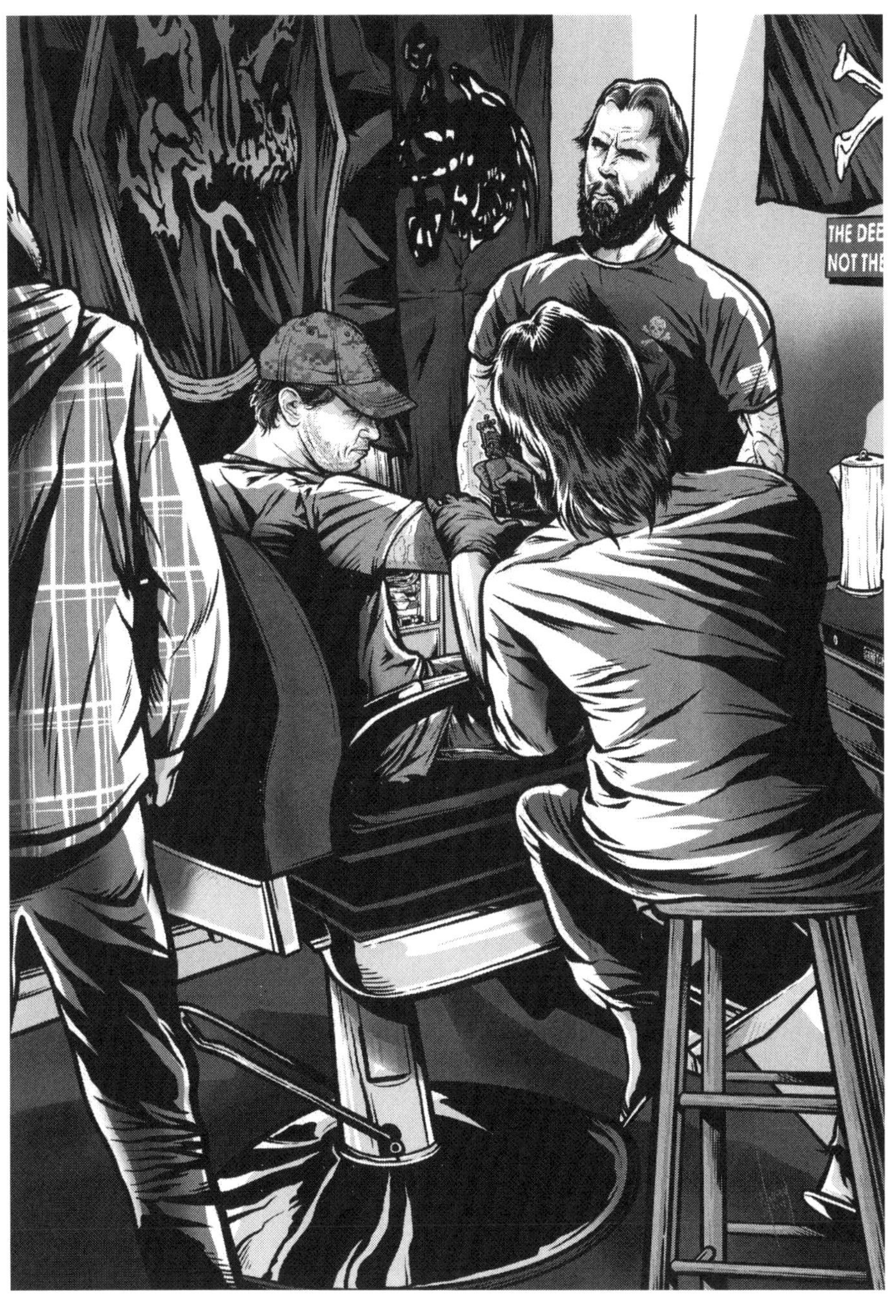

I got home late and stayed up flipping through the Bible. Leslie woke up and nudged me, "Babe, what are you doing?"

"I'm just trying to wrap my mind around everything. For some people, their faith is just words on a page, ideas they like the sound of enough to believe in, but it's fake. It's become very real for me, my faith in God."

She looked at me, sat up and rubbed her eyes. "What do you mean 'real?' Like how?"

"I mean, it's always been there but, being in combat, seeing that kind of thing, doing the things I did, it's different."

"I think I understand what you mean," she said, "like He's truly there with you?"

I said, "Exactly. Like I know He is there with me every time."

We looked at each other for a moment and considered each other. I wasn't always there for her. Just because I was home didn't mean everything was perfect. We did our best to spend time together but I was seldom home, even when we weren't deployed. We were constantly training for anything, for everything. Then we'd leave for war again.

She reached over and put her hand on my arm and closed her eyes. I kept reading and started thinking about the next deployment. We'd be going to Iraq this time and I knew it was game on from the stories of the guys that were there. It was a slayfest of Al-Qaida, plus we couldn't wait for a change of scenery from Afghanistan.

We had a bad-ass flight crew on the C-17 ride over to Al Asad, Iraq. Guys were racked out all over the ISUs and had their hammocks strung up and gently swaying in the belly of the aircraft. Guys were listening to iPods and reading with headlamps.

I opened my Bible back up to Romans, Chapter 8. Noah was next to me.

"Whatcha reading, bro?"

I crunched an Ambien, swallowed it and began to read out loud for him. "There is therefore now no condemnation to those who are in

Christ Jesus, who do not walk after the flesh, but after the spirit."

I looked back over at him and had already lost his attention. The sluggish feeling of the Ambien started to come over me and my eyes got heavy. All that was left was the ambient rumble of the plane's engines, quiet and calm. A final breath before the storm.

After a long flight and layover in Germany, we finally arrived at Al Asad, Iraq and the first thing I noticed was that it was nighttime and cold. It was always hard when we showed up to a new place at night. It takes a minute to get your bearings and figure out where the essential stuff is like chow hall, ready room, flight line and, most important, the gym. The outgoing Team turned over new SOPs (Standard Operating Procedures) that had changed during their deployment.

As the sun started its way back up in the sky I could feel the temperature rising fast. I walked outside the slumlord palace we lived in and all I could see was a brown hue of the dirty air and a constant smell of burning trash that was vastly different than the scene of endless mountains in Afghanistan.

I didn't think anything could look and feel shittier than southern Afghanistan. I was wrong. This place looked and felt like you'd imagine if the sun had an ass and you lived in the hole. Of course I hadn't been to Somalia yet. That shithole takes the cake as the world's sewer.

As usual, we got our kit sorted and I went to our room to claim a bed and a home for the next four months. Out at the fire pit, I walked up next to Gold Dust and Medlow, who were having a beer and turning over with the outgoing Team. Medlow took a monster hit off the hooka and yelled," I am immortal!" while smoke billowed out of his mouth.

I looked at Gold Dust. "What do I gotta do to go to Recce, bro? You know I want to be with the snipers."

Gold Dust sipped his beer, "Sheff, I already told you not to worry about that right now. This is only your second pump with Blue. You're about to be breaching your ass off."

I stared into the flames and pulled hard off the hookah.

"Your mom's gonna get a second pump," I mumbled, chuckling to myself. "But seriously, bro, please don't mess with me. Can I at least start planning routes with you guys?" I begged.

Gold Dust looked over at Johnny, who was sippin' on his Jack. "I don't care. He can if he wants to."

Johnny looked at me and said, "I don't care if you start walking up front with the point element, but you still need to breach and clear with the guys. Then, if they need or want you for overwatch or whatever, you can go. We'll see how it goes after a few. Cool?"

I was pumped. I had an in. I wanted to be with Recce bad. They were always in the action.

The first target we hit was in the middle of Fallujah, an urban area with street lights. Me and Shane moved up to the primary entry point and the Team stacked up in the shadows behind cover, holding on all possible threats. I placed a strip charge on the door over the locking mechanism and capped in. As we slowly moved back, I unreeled enough shock tube to get around the corner and then there was movement inside.

Gold Dust was on a building adjacent and he took aim at one unknown, silhouetted in a top floor window.

Sonny's voice came over the radio in a whisper.

"Standby…Three…Two…One…Execute…Execute…Execute!"

On the first execute, the snipers went hot on four guys, roof top, dropping all four of them.

The second execute was my cue. I pressed the release trigger on my duel-primed shooter and the door exploded into pieces, blowing it in and out of the way.

I made entry and looked down the hallway. A fighter had come out with a female in front of him. Her arms were up.

"Fuck me."

The enemy fighter began shooting from behind her down the hallway and I sucked back out of the way and got as small as possible in a side room doorway. I put my laser on his chest. Shane was yelling at him in Arabic to drop his gun and release the girl. The female's arm was still in the way but I let one rip right through it. She screamed as the bad guy behind her crumpled to the ground. He was still moving around and twitching. I got the injured woman to come to me and got her into a room.

"Get the dog up here!" Shane yelled.

Our dog came in like a bullet and latched on to the dude's face and literally dragged this guy by his skull, back past us and out of the building. I could see his head coming apart. I looked over the female's arm. She had a superficial flesh wound and she actually thanked me while crying and dribbling.

"Last room. All clear."

Sonny came over comms a few minutes later, "2-Troop, this is 2-2. Target SECURE, let's get a hasty SSE. Nuke-1, how we looking?

Nuke-1 was our EOD guy. He was already placing charges on a pile of weapons and ordnance that was found on target.

"2-2, this is Nuke-1. Charges set. Timers set for 10 mikes, OVER."

Nuke-1, this is 2-2, ROGER. BREAK. All stations, police up your shit. Target secure. Leave nothing for the Haj. We're dropping the building."

On the way out to the HLZ, we had all the bad guys that weren't dead lined up, cuffed and hooded. We turned the prisoners toward the building and pulled their hoods up so they could see.

Over comms, "All Stations, Nuke-1, Standby. Fire in the hole!"

We all watched together like a happy family roasting marshmallows at the campfire. The building went in high order in an explosion that lit up the whole area.

The next morning, I saw Shane and some of the others heading to breakfast.

"Hey, Sheff, you coming with?"

"Na," I said, "I'm good. I'm gonna start looking at routes."

"Chugger…"

"I'll be in the Recce Hooch, faggots."

I walked into the snipers' planning area. There were white Christmas lights strung all around to barely illuminate the room. It was some real underworld shit. There was a large Bones flag on the wall, and flat screens showing different ISR feeds and different overhead imagery covered the rest of the walls. These guys kept their fingers on the pulse of every detail.

I looked around the room. A couple of guys were already planning for the next target. There was a long L-shaped couch and a coffee table with a candle going next to a large hookah. I could faintly hear Tool on a speaker turned way low. They looked up at me, "What's up, Gaylord, you lost, bro?"

I kinda laughed it off. "I just want to watch you guys do the route."

Gold Dust motioned me over, "He's just messing with you, Sheff, don't start getting all emotional on us already. You can practice right here."

They gave me my own set-up, so I'd go in every day and try to mirror whatever they were doing with their route planning. I realized how much went into planning. It didn't take long, though, and I was planning better routes faster than these Jabronis that were there before me.

Military Google Earth had a yellow spinning globe instead of a blue one. It was incredibly detailed and, if the settings were set properly, we could match terrain features almost exactly. This was key when detailing a difficult route for guys to see beforehand. There was also an extensive and elaborate database of former fighter camps, IED attacks, mine fields, and so on. On another screen, I saw a satellite photo of some forty square miles that I was able to zoom in down to a small rock. I sat there and just took it in for a minute. They hadn't fully accepted me yet but I knew, at this point, if I didn't mess up, they would. A couple pilots came in and sat on the couch and talked with the other snipers. They were wearing tan flight suits. TF Brown was the Helo Squadron we flew with. They are among the best pilots in the world.

Next to the door I saw an ammo can with the lid removed and on the side it read "Assaulter GPSs" and it was filled with wristwatch-style Garmins. Guys would drop them off to get the route loaded for the night's mission.

That night was the first night I was up front with the other snipers. I had a position in Recce and I was really nervous about getting it right. The walk in to the target was uneventful. The terrain was mostly flat except for the occasional irrigation ditches crisscrossing the dusty Iraqi landscape. The air was hot and carried a smell of body odor and burning trash. I'll never forget the smell of that place.

We arrived at ORP, and I moved out to the target building with the snipers to set containment. I moved into position and set my ladder. I climbed up on the wall and took up my position. The comms piece in my ear crackled when Gold Dust passed the word.

"2-2, India-1, Recce is set."

"Roger India-1, BREAK…2 Troop, commence assault."

The assaulters started moving and immediately some dog started going ape-shit. I was looking through this little window into the structure, and I remember just seeing the slightest movement. The Assault Team got up to us and the Entry Team started stacking on the gate. As soon as they started to move the latch on that shitty old metal gate, the front door erupted. AK fire immediately started ripping through the door and hitting randomly around all of us. I crouched behind the wall and peeked through a little hole into the compound.

"2-Troop, hold what you got. India-1, how many shooters?"

Gold Dust keyed up, "2-2, I count three…"

And the shooting started again. Two guys ran out from a side door. One was firing an AK in our direction and the other ran behind him and shouldered his RPG. I heard the familiar "tshh-tshhh" of our suppressed weapons and they were both down.

This other guy came out and he had a little kid in front of him with his little hands up. I was still up on my ladder and peering through this little rubbled-out hole in the wall with my night vision. I could see him and he started shooting from over this boy's shoulder at the gate where the assaulters were.

I crouched on the top of my ladder with my gun up over my head over the wall. And I was like "I gotta hit this dude, right behind this kid. Don't mess this up." I got my laser lined up, gun sideways," and I was like "tshh-tshh" and I dropped him.

The boy's little hands were up and my rounds went right past his arm. I hit this asshole in the chest, hit him again, and he fell. Another guy came out and grabbed the AK. As soon as he got out of view of the kid, I shot him, too. This poor little kid was just standing there screaming and crying. I'll never forget it.

Meanwhile, there was another dude taking aim at me. He was on the roof. I didn't see him because I was dealing with this, and Shane drilled him.

"Holy shit, thank you, bro," I yelled out.

"Hell, yeah, bro," he said. "Let's go get the leftovers, too."

Gold Dust came over comms, "2-Troop, you're good to move. BREAK. Sheff, you can clear with assault."

We went down inside and cleared through. I didn't shoot anybody else but outside we got word that things were getting sporty.

"2-Troop, 2-2, target secure, hasty SSE, get a head count and get ready to move."

So we started gathering what we could and getting ready to move. But one dude wasn't dead. He was lying there doing his gurgle. He was there dying, and our dumb shit of a commander called for a CASEVAC for like fifteen Humvees. This was the first and last op he went on with us.

"2-Troop, this is 2-1. Belay that last transmission." This cake-eating clownshoe 0-3 was always extra-proper with his radio calls, a proper douche.

"Uniform-1, make the call. I want CASEVAC for this wounded."

We stood there in disbelief. He was calling them to come out and do a Casualty EVAC for this dude. So we're like, "Wait, hold on—we're gonna bring a convoy into this area of people to CAS EVAC this guy? This is retarded."

We ended up having to wagon-wheel the whole troop on top of about four rooftops because we started taking effective fire from nearly three-hundred-sixty degrees while we were waiting for this idiot commander to get this dying bad guy out.

Needless to say, the asshole in the compound finally died, thank God, and we canceled the convoy.

We went out damned near every night and damned near every night got into a gunfight with the enemy. From room-to-room close quarters, to full-on land warfare-style combat, we were doing everything we had learned in training. But the enemy still got a vote.

Another night, on some other target, a guy came out spraying lead and some of the guys stacked up outside got hit bad. I was a little concerned about my buddy who was down, shot through both legs. One of our Rangers got hit in leg out on the blocking position as well. But we just kept going, win the fight, tend to the wounded, EXFIL, rejock and refit, and go back out. It was like this non-stop war party going on. And everybody had their own little piece to deal with.

It was dirty and it was grimy and we were trying to just live through it and be pros. By that time, we had lost several guys and we could feel the separation of what used to be normal. I loved being with my Team but I couldn't wait to get home.

We finished that deployment with more than a hundred missions under our belts, having killed hundreds of Al-Qaeda. MOB VI had earned a sinister reputation as the painted warriors. I had lots of practice walking point, blowing doors in, and especially killing the enemy. It was starting to make sense to me. This was who I was to be and I enjoyed being relied on.

Chapter 10

NO QUARTER

Then, just like that, I was home again, expected to be a regular guy, be a husband, mow the yard, go to church, smile, whatever. We were required to see a psychiatrist post-deployment. And, when people started dying and the funerals started, they told us, "Guys, you gotta go see the shrink. And we were like, "Dude, we're fine."

We would debrief our required sessions with the command shrinks among each other. We'd ask each other things like, "Hey, did he ask you if you've ever killed anybody? What'd you say? Yeah. Did he ask you if it bothered you or shit like that?" We were terrified to be honest because we thought that, if they found out something was wrong with us, they would remove us from the Team. And then what? That was more terrifying, because I didn't really know what else to do.

There was a sheet that we'd fill out with questions like: Were you in close proximity to a gun fight? Did you see anyone killed? Did anyone you know get hurt? Injured? Shot? Blown up? Anyone that you know or anyone close to you killed? How is your sleep?

They'd always ask, "How's your drinking?"

"It's fine."

"How many drinks do you think you have in a week?"

"I don't know, as many as the next guy."

"Well, what does that mean? Just give us a baseline."

And we knew already if our answer was more than six drinks a day, you're gonna be considered an alcoholic. We had this little diagram: If you have this many drinks, you're an alcoholic kind of thing.

Look, apart from combat, every single block of training we did together carried the potential for guys to get killed, and sometimes they did. So opportunities to celebrate our time together as a Team and a family did not go unused. And, like everything else we did, it was max effort. Usually the guys would come over to my house and we'd sit on my back deck and tell stories and listen to music until the sun came up. Good times.

The pace was hard sometimes on the home life but I loved spending time with Leslie when I was home. She was always supportive of me and she always encouraged me to continue in the Teams as long as I was happy. She never failed to pray for me and my Team when we were away.

Our short work-up started with us training and re-training new tactics we'd derived from the previous deployments and real world experience with the enemy. We continued to evolve as a force and it was evident in the training that my Team was getting to a point where we were simply reading off one another without saying a word. The efficiency was like nothing I'd ever seen. Everything we did was serious and with a purpose.

Soon, we'd deploy again. I'd be going back to Afghanistan, this time as a recce sniper and point man. I was thrilled. That's what I had wanted since I got my trident. To me, it was the ultimate. We were heavily relied on during all phases of the mission and being in the know was critical to success. We'd be tasked with planning the routes and the HLZs, which meant waking up earlier than the others most of the time to watch ISR feeds and study targets. We would always work directly with intel and the pilots. It was our job, yes, but being in the know all the time for me in that environment was clutch.

It became a routine almost. We said our goodbyes at the fence.

We loaded the plane and the next thing I knew we were touching down on the tarmac in Bagram. Welcome back. I knew the war was on. I got off the plane and looked around at the ever-expanding BAF. It had turned into a city. I smiled. I was happy to be back.

A group of SEALs gathered in the Recce Hooch, poring over maps, GRG projections, satellite imagery and among them were Medlow and Eric the prick.

"What's up, Medlow?" I gave him a hug and flipped Eric off.

They had both switched to another squadron and were heading back home.

"Whadda ya got, fellas, I heard the shit was on!"

Medlow looked at me. "Sheff, I'm just glad we're headed home and y'all can take this mess off our hands."

I looked on the screen at the satellite imagery and saw a small village positioned high up in a bowl on the top of some mountains in the Wagal Valley. Wataper, Wagal and Kunar were valleys to not dick around in. I hadn't been up in there since the buffoonery days at Seal Team Eight when we'd go up in the daytime. We didn't know any better at that time.

Eric bumps me, "Hey, all bullshit aside, it's a nightmare up there, man. The terrain is pretty gnarly. We got lit up trying to come in from the low ground. We've been after this guy for a couple of months and unable to get him. He's one of bin Laden's guys."

Me and Gold Dust and a couple other guys started looking at everything we could get our hands on. I was looking at high ground to come in from, but the hump in would be pretty epic.

Gold Dust was skeptical. "The terrain looks really bad, but you know what, Sheff, you gotta pop your cherry sometime. Welcome to Recce. Enjoy!"

My mind was already spinning. I knew we could do it. If bad guys lived up there, they had to get up there somehow, I thought.

"Hey, brother, can we take the helos out in the day time and actually get eyes on it? Maybe the bad guys will just think it's just another ring flight as long as we stay in the big open valleys. I'll videotape it and we can compare with Google."

Gold Dust looked at me for a second. "I like it, Sheff. Let's do it. Plan it out."

After about an hour ride from BAF, we were in pocket over some nasty mountains. I used an old Sony Handy Cam, like the kind we used at Medlow's mother's house. We got back and reviewed the footage and then matched it with Google Earth, looking at the mountains on the GRG. I pointed to the screen.

"What about right here? Land them here or it'd be a short fast rope." I pointed to what appeared to be an opening on the ridgeline at about nine thousand feet in a saddle.

Gold Dust looked skeptical. "And then what, Sheff, climb? You crazy?"

We all jocked up in full kit and met in the gym by the scale to take weights. They had to be precise for the helos. Every ounce matters at that altitude. The birds have trouble carrying a lot of weight and maneuvering at those elevations.

Noah stepped up to the scale and got on.

"Two point four pounds over the limit, bro. Lose something."

"Maybe don't eat any pop tarts for a few days. Your mother's two pounds over the limit as well, Noah," Shane yelled from the back.

We all ended up dropping our normal plates and wearing smaller chicken plates, we called them. They were a bit lighter and basically cover your heart. I was wearing my approach shoes, which are climbing shoes you can run in. I had on lightweight pants and a t-shirt. I had a helmet, my radio, my NODS, my HK M4, and my Sig Sauer 239 with hollow points, as well as four M4 mags loaded out with .77 grain Black Hills, a bottle of water, and a can of Copenhagen.

As soon as everyone dumped their excess gear, we hopped into the helo for the night flight to the drop point, passing JBAD on the way in. We could see the lights blinking far below, like little green fireflies. There were eighteen of us in the chopper, including Blue Team, six Army Rangers, four Afghani troops, and an interpreter.

The helos reached the drop point, gave us thirty seconds to scramble, then left us in the pitch black and roared off. We began to climb. I was up front with Johnny and Gold Dust—I was the lead. We'd be climbing up over twelve thousand feet, so it all mattered. The route was the route.

We began movement and had to stow away rifles on our backs and climb. Three points of contact traverse. We brought a small climber's set-up with some cams and safety rope for guys to clip in and out of. It was one of those climbs where I was glad I was on NVGs because I couldn't actually see how steep the terrain was.

I was thinking to myself, Sweet, I'm gonna die over here at war, falling off a mountain.

We continued to make our way up in single file and, from time to time, I'd stop, take my eyes off the narrow trail, and study the surrounding terrain. It was oddly beautiful. On one side, we were looking out over Afghanistan, at those immense, spectacular mountains, lit up by the moon and stars, everything crystal clear in that thin air and at that high altitude. In the other direction, looking toward Pakistan, I could see city lights glowing in the distance, and the contrast between the two vistas was otherworldly. I was glad I was looking through my NVGs at a screen, because it didn't seem real, and to have looked at it with my own eyes might have made me question my sanity.

Johnny inserted a small climbing cam into the rock face we were traversing and climbed on ahead. As long as he didn't fall, we'd be good. He was setting the safety up.

I climbed out a ways and looked back. Guys were strung out all the way down the ridgeline, slowly climbing to us. I could see the top but it was still so far off. As long as we could make it by sun-up and have the target surrounded, we'd have the upper hand. Maybe. That's what we were banking on and praying for.

We almost bit off more than we could chew on that route but, five hours in, we made it to the peak of the mountain we were going over. We had another seven kilometers to go but it was mostly downhill and a walk in the park compared to that climb we'd just done.

Johnny came over near the edge where I was. "Hey, bro, look at those Dall sheep." He pointed at the herd passing through. "I wish we could just shoot that big one and come get them later."

The guys were still climbing up to us and they were lagging behind. "Hey, Johnny, what the hell are they doing back there?"

He keyed the radio. "Hey, 2-Troop, let's go. Tighten it up."

I keyed my own radio. "Slasher-91, this is Juliet-2 Interrogative. Any movement on target at this time? OVER."

"Juliet-2, this is Slasher-91, ROGER. No movement at this time. OVER."

"ROGER. Juliet-2 OUT."

We finally all made it up the mountain and established a perimeter on top. We gave the guys ten minutes to get some water and rest. The sweat on my shirt was starting to freeze solid. Everyone was sucking air. That was the problem living at two thousand feet in JBAD and operating up over ten thousand feet. We had to stay in Gym Jones shape.

This target was Objective Smoke Screen. He had some Haj name that probably started with something sounding a lot like Mohammad. Just a guess.

He was supposedly linked to bin Laden somehow but was unattainable.

We tightened our approach shoes up and made it down to the target area in about two hours. We had about thirty minutes of nighttime left before these guys could see how big of a force we weren't.

I was up front walking down the mountain on the ridgeline trail. I could see through the huge redwood trees and was starting to make out structures down below.

Shane came up alongside me, "You see anything?"

I scanned with my thermal scope. It looked like a Tibetan village high up on the side of these mountains that were connected by this bowl that sat around eight thousand feet.

"Stand fast," I whispered into my radio.

Everyone stopped. The whole line stopped and I looked back to the sight of green eyes coming down the mountain like a line of predators. I could see someone standing in our path looking up at us.

"Recce's taking shots," I whispered into my mike. I breathed in and out and rolled off safety. I had my crosshair on this first guy's chest and squeezed two rounds.

THWAP-THWAP.

I waited a second and then dropped his buddy. "2-Troop, Juliet-2, 2 EKIA, moving forward. All clear."

Without another word, the patrol continued creeping forward like creatures from the Black Lagoon. I stepped over the two bodies. The one had come up just as I squeezed on the other. God's timing never fails. I sparkled the target with my infra-red laser and the guys moved to the target building and set containment.

Me and Gold Dust moved up and climbed on the main target building to provide overwatch while the Team moved to the entry. It was a soft entry. As we crested the roof, I looked to my right and I saw three enemy fighters sleeping on the roof, next to their guns. Gold Dust very quietly and meticulously climbed up next to me and raised his rifle.

"On you," he whispered.

As soon as he said it, I face-shot the first guy and we crisscrossed these dudes like Swiss cheese. Rounds zipped through these fighters, sending them straight to hell.

The main door was barricaded so Shane placed a charge on the door. When it blew, I could hear muffled gunfire erupt from inside. Then the whole target broke loose. We were engaging multiple fighters coming down from high ground positions marked by the aircraft. They were sparkling all movers for us. Then the Assault Team started making calls over comms.

"2-2, this is Echo-2…hot hallway, barricaded shooter. Multiple squirters out the east side building 1-1. BREAK…Recce, how we looking?"

"Echo-2, this is Juliet-2, ROGER that we are working it. OVER."

Then I heard, "RPG!"

An RPG whistled past inches from me. Me and Gold Dust lay flat.

"Holy shit, that was close!"

"Hey, man, I think they know we're up here."

Gold Dust laughed. "Nah, probably just a lucky shot or an accident."

I looked over the edge of the rooftop and saw another fighter maneuvering to fire another RPG at us. I held my rifle level and put my laser on his face, rolled off my safety, and squeezed the trigger twice, sending two shots back to back.

He spun as the rounds impacted his chest and then he shot the RPG into the ground in the courtyard. It didn't go, too short to arm. PKM tracer rounds came sailing in from another compound. It looked like a river of light. The whole bowl was now in multiple engagements. The Ranger-blocking positions we had dropped off on the high ground were fully engaging fighters from other compounds.

"Johnny, you think we can get some bombs on these guys?"

Rounds were ripping through the courtyard at full auto.

Johnny looked up at me, "Working on it, bro. Uniform-1, Echo-1."

"Echo-1, go for Uniform-1."

"Contact building 6-1,6-3 and we got multiples moving in the open, north of building 1-1, maybe five hundred meters. They're heading to high ground. OVER."

"ROGER that, Echo-1…tracking all. Standby for fire mission"

It was mayhem. Everyone was getting some. Fighters were coming out from other buildings into the open and yelling at each other, trying to organize. It was all we could do to keep them at bay.

Me and Gold Dust crawled on our backs to the edge of the roof because we were getting lit up from the high ground again. We both bailed off the roof into the courtyard below and made a break for the gate.

Guys were still getting it on internal as well. It was a maze with armed bad guys around damned near every corner.

Gold Dust keyed up his comms. "Echo-2, this is Juliet-1. Recce is displaced at this time, moving to rooftop building 1-2-0. How copy, OVER?"

Shane keyed up. "Good copy…we're target secure building 1-1. Echo is moving external at this time. BREAK…2-2, Echo-2…Can we get the dog up to our location? Courtyard building 1-1. OVER."

"Echo-2, this is 2-2. Standby. Xray-1 is moving to your location at this time. BREAK…Juliet-1…2-2. Let me know when you guys are set. We're getting ready to drop bombs."

I heard automatic gunfire where Echo Team was.

"2-2, this is Echo-2… Eagle down, Ambulatory. Papa-1 is working on him now. ROGER, Echo-2."

Then I heard Medlow key up, "BREAK, BREAK, BREAK…Echo-2, Delta-2, multiple fighters moving external building 1-1 trying to gain entry. Delta-1 is hit. Push Papa-1 when able."

"ROGER, Delta-2, what's your location? Papa-1 is moving now."

Me and Gold Dust moved external to the target building. As we stepped out into the alleyway, Johnny covered our movement. He rounded the corner and there was a bad guy right there that grabbed his rifle. They briefly wrestled back and forth, then Johnny hip-tossed the guy against the mud wall. No sooner did his body hit the dirt than Johnny had pasted his brains on the wall, dumping three hollow-point .45 ACP rounds through his forehead.

Another guy poked his head out from a rooftop and I could see a barrel. Me and Gold Dust matched lasers on his face and shot the top of his head clean off. His eyeballs were hanging out and he slid off the building and landed at my feet, making a gurgling noise. It was really gross.

I keyed my mike, "2-2, this is Juliet-2. Climbing building 1-2-0 at this time, OVER."

"ROGER, Juliet-2…BREAK…All stations be advised, Slasher-91 inbound with 40mm and 105s on multiple movers in the open. We got a pack of fifteen and a pack of eight."

I heard the C-130 engines roaring as the bird broke hard right into its orbit, banking over the ridge and raining down a firestorm of 40mm grenades. It sounded like thunder.

There was nothing left of the bad guys.

The fire became sporadic and dying out. In all the excitement, Nicky got hit twice through the trap and was sitting over in the doorway keeping pressure on his blowout. Boyd waited on the Tango, who wasn't dead yet. He was lying there doing his death gurgle from being throat-shot.

Barry stacked all the weapons in a pile, then went to one of the Tangos and pulled his chest rack. He had to flip out his blade and cut it free. He threw it on the pile.

I stared down at the guy dying. I watched the life leave him.

"2-Troop, this is Echo-1, target secure building 1-1, 1-2, and 1-4. The dog took a round. Nuke-1 is setting charges at this time."

"Echo-1...2-2, ROGER. Copy all. Let us know what you need down there. BREAK...BREAK...Delta-2, how we looking?"

Medlow keyed his radio, "Papa-1 is working on him but we're gonna need the stretcher over here."

I could see Sonny up there in the C2 element working air support still.

Sonny came back over comms, "Roger that, Delta-2, I'm sending the litter now. BREAK...Recce, this is 2-2. How we looking?"

Gold Dust, peering through his thermal scope, keyed his mike, "ROGER...we got four MAMs, internal building 4-1. No threat at this time. Other than that we're all quiet...Standby..."

THWAP, THWAP.

"Make that two MAMs internal building 4-1. OVER."

"2-Troop, this is 2-2, prep for EXFIL. Recce has an HLZ but we gotta climb back up to it. We got about fifteen mikes until the sun starts up. Let's move!"

It was some epic flying by TF Brown. They backed that bus in so the ramp only touched the ridgeline we were on, and we all hauled ass on as they hovered.

After we had inserted, it had taken a thousand feet, twelve hours of climbing and forty-three enemy dead before we were high and dry and headed back to JBAD. I was looking forward to a shower and some sleep.

It became carnage like that night after night. A chaplain who stayed with us started praying over us every night before we went out. I said so many prayers that deployment on my own, I started wondering if God was tired of hearing my voice.

We caused absolute chaos for the enemy. An enemy report from a Taliban leader came in to our Intel people that read:

> *There's a new special type of foot soldier on the battlefield. One who comes in the night. They are painted and have beards and green eyes. They bring lions with them. DO not fight them. They will kill you all. Run to Pakistan. Get out of here if you want to live.*

All I could think was, Message sent, Message received… NO QUARTER."

This was war, this was combat, and it came with a price. The very thing that drove us to win was the same thing that was taking over at home. We were looking forward to the combat above all else.

Chapter 11
GODSPEED

"Good route, last night, bro."

Johnny walked over and slapped me on the shoulder. We were in the ready room stowing away gear and rejocking for the next night. I changed out all my batteries and cleaned my weapon. Then I reloaded my magazines and grabbed a couple of frags. The rest of my kit was ready to assault.

Johnny was getting his normal plates ready again and he said, "Hey, bro, ICOM chatter sounds like we got our guy last night. By the way, you need to go call Sonny. He's already headed back to BAF with the birds. Something about a low vis op in Kabul with OGA. They needed a Recce guy. You're going."

"Well, okay, then. I guess I'll go call the master chief. What will you guys do without me though? Hahaha."

"I think we'll be fine, asshole."

I made a quick call and got my marching orders. I linked up with these CIA guys at a secret base on an undisclosed location a day later. I could see why they asked for help. This was some real amateur hour-type shit. They'd roll around in the daytime with a very small crew in crappy vans that look like locals. In my jammies with my beard and head wrap, I could pass for an Arab, so I loaded up with them and headed out for one of these snatch-and-grab ops.

Kabul was another shithole. It was a string of dilapidated buildings, open fields, and millions of people who seemed to wander mindlessly. We did the same thing every day. We'd drive around doing reconnaissance and surveillance and try to pinpoint locations of where the bad guys were. We'd either snatch the turds right off the street or out of their houses. Or we would wait until night, keeping eyes on and then hit them with an overt assault force.

The OGA guy rode with his laptop out and open in the back of the VW van. We'd keep the curtains closed as much as possible and bring extra wool blankets to hide our plates and weapons under our feet. This would fool the corrupt dickheads at the checkpoints for a while, but eventually we were starting to get some weird looks. I spoke up at the next brief and looked at the chief of base, who was this heavyset fella behind a desk. He couldn't care less about war.

"Look, I'm uncomfortable going out in the day in some of these areas because we're getting a lot of looks. I feel like something is going to happen. We're not getting away with this much longer."

"Well, Sheff, we'll have the QRF standing by here to respond if something happens to you. You're not scared, are you?"

I almost threw up in my mouth. I looked him right in the eyes.

"No offense, bro, but this is Kabul. That's not gonna work for us. I want the QRF no farther than a click away, please. I'm sure you understand."

"Okay, that's fine. We can set up a Vehicle Checkpoint here. Will that work?"

He pointed to a small area in the target AO on the massive map on the wall.

I looked at where they were looking and where we would be operating.

"Okay, that works for us. Just do me a favor and send me a grid when you get set up."

"Okay, let's roll in an hour," he said.

I went over to the Morale Welfare and Recreation (MWR) building. It had a theater set up with a couch and a couple of computers. There was a phone to call home in a booth off to the side. I hadn't called Leslie yet and it had already been several weeks. I knew I needed to check in.

I called and she answered immediately, crying. "Babe, thank God, I needed to talk to you so bad. I have to tell you something," she said, "I'm pregnant."

"You're pregnant?"

"Yes, three months…I found out after you left but I hadn't gotten the chance to talk to you yet. Are you okay?"

I tried not to break down right there, "Yes, Babe, I'm good to go. We're gonna do this, okay? Don't worry. We're gonna be together. I'm excited. What is it? Holy shit! I'm gonna be a dad."

I heard her laughing and crying but she sounded relieved. Marriage was tough sometimes. It had its ups and downs. We had to work at it. I was pretty rough around the edges and sometimes short-tempered. So that didn't help much. But, like everything else, the Lord carried us.

I sat back in the chair and couldn't think about what we were about to do. I just wondered what he would look like. Obviously, I knew it would be a man-child.

I walked over to the fridge and opened the freezer. There sat a bottle of ice-cold Jack. I took a swill. Then I went and donned my man jammies and got all Haji'd out. We loaded up in the vans and passed all the gun trucks that were standing by to head out and set up a checkpoint.

We still had about three hours of daylight left.

Once we rolled into the area, our Afghan driver Salim pulled the vehicle over and parked in a busy area. The Ground Branch guy had his laptop open and was waiting for a ping. He was in the middle seat and me and Marco were in the back.

The Ground Branch guy saw some guy come out of store with a profile that matched his target.

"That's him!" he told Salim. "That's him. Long white robe!"

Salim was already on his radio telling the Team to move in on the walker.

Our Afghan operatives walked up behind the target and grabbed an arm on each side while whispering into his ear in Pashto, "Don't do anything. Get into the car. Don't try to resist!"

They manhandled this older-looking Afghan to a car with its door open. When they got close to pushing him in, he freaked out and started screaming, making a huge scene.

An Afghan cop that was hanging on to the back of a Jenga bus was cruising by at the worst possible time. I was watching him.

"Okay, fellas, that turd is on his radio already," I said. "We need to move now before this place is swarming."

I didn't know a lot about where we were, but I did know the cops were about as corrupt as the Muslims we were fighting. Another vehicle full of police in mismatched uniforms pulled up. There were at least ten cops now, all wielding AKs. Immediately, another vehicle cut us off. They had blocked us in on the front and back. I guess one of the younger cops had made us through the windows.

"I knew this would happen," I muttered.

Marco leaned over to me, "What do we do, bro?"

The OGA guy up front started yelling like a badass, "Do you know who we are?"

I looked all around us. The situation was going from bad to worse. I tried to calm us down.

"Everyone just stay calm for now. We don't need big balls right now. We need to be cool, please."

I looked at Marco and could see the color leaving his face. Then I grabbed the GPS we had shoved up in the roof. I was praying it had a good signal. I started giving direction.

"Hey, man, if we have to get out of this vehicle, I'm gonna start shooting counter clockwise and you start shooting clockwise. We'll take as many of them out as we can."

He immediately answered, "I'm down, man, say when!"

I yelled up from the back to Salim, "Hey, bro, what are they yelling out there?"

"Mister Sheff, there is a riot forming from the people. They know we have Americans in here. The cops are saying they are going to kill us here on the street. What should we do, sir?"

I looked out and tried to see behind me while I keyed the radio to try to get some help. Comms were spotty at best inside the city so I diverted to my Haji cellphone. The phone was unsecure, but this was an emergency. I couldn't get through, and I couldn't see the street anymore because there were so many people pouring out. Bricks and rocks started coming in hot and I could hear and feel large bricks hitting the van.

I tried the radio again, "Alpha 9-9, Alpha 9-9, this Omega 9-1, OVER."

"Omega 9-1, this Alpha 9-9, ROGER OVER. Standing by."

About time, I thought as I keyed up again,

"Alpha 9-9, troops in contact. Troops in contact. Standby for grid. BREAK."

"Alpha 9-9…Omega 9-1, grid as follows Forty Two Sierra Whiskey Delta, 6-9-8-5-4…4-3-3-1-7…BREAK…Requesting QRF at this time. Please confirm location OVER."

"Omega 9-1, ROGER copy. Sending the QRF at this time. They're forty minutes out."

They were spinning the Ranger QRF in BAF up for us. My guys at the vehicle check point had been dispatched as well but were having trouble making it through the mob. They were still at least fifteen minutes from us. In fifteen minutes we'd all be dead. It went back and forth in my mind, Do I just pick up the gun and start shooting as many as I can? I can't just let myself die here, I thought.

The one who appeared to be in charge came up to our van. He was pointing at me and yelling to his guys. There were no less than ten AKs pointed at our vehicle now. They had their filthy fingers on the triggers and their safeties off. The only thing to separate us was a pane of glass.

I looked out the front of the vehicle and could see that the sun was setting and illuminating the total fog of street dust. I said a prayer to the Lord for deliverance and protection. I hadn't realized I was praying out loud, and I think it freaked Marco out.

Then, all of the sudden, there were flashes of bright red light everywhere. The adrenaline was rolling and I thought for a second, I've been shot and I'm dying now.

But it was the Afghan QRF. They had made a wake through the crowd for us. I started to make out HUMVEEs and Toyota gun trucks and they were ramming through traffic, knocking vehicles out of the way. Guys were up on top of the vehicles with their overt red lasers activated.

They were face-shining anyone in their path and yelling at them, "BACK THE FUCK UP!"

I almost started clapping and yelled out, "Yes, thank God!"

We hooded the guy in charge as well as the bad guy we were after. Then, after stuffing them in the back of a couple of trucks, we hauled ass back to the base in what felt like a high-speed pursuit. I had already changed out of my man jammies and put my plates on and my weapon at the ready. I was looking to roll back out there proper and finish what we'd started, but there was a call for me inside, apparently urgent.

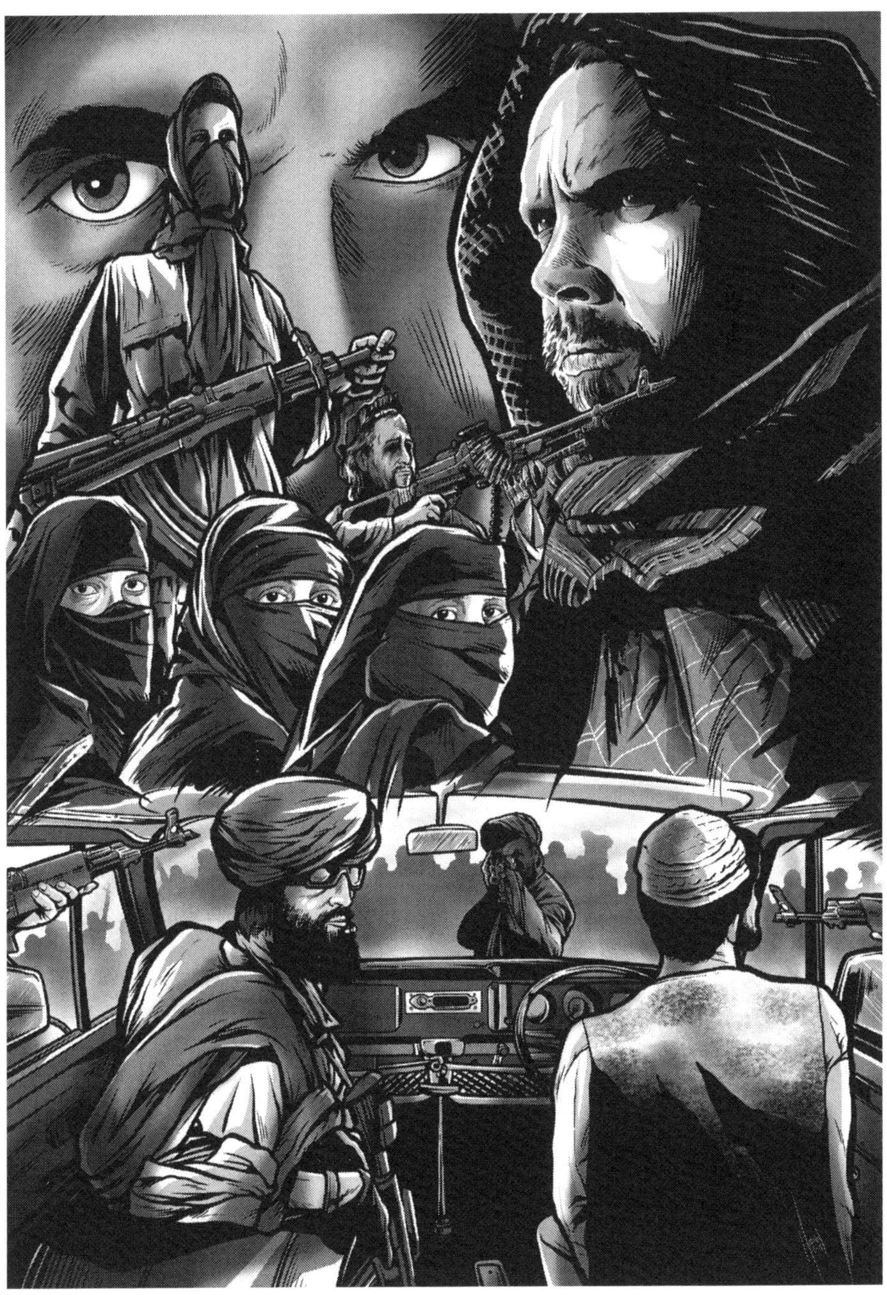

I got out of my truck and headed back into the SCIF. I picked up the red phone. It was Shane.

"Hey, man, you okay?"

"Yeah, bro, good to hear your voice. That sucked!"

Shane said, "We are about to be flying to BAF to refuel before hitting a target over in your neck of the woods. Johnny said you're on the bird if you can make it in time."

I did the math. By the time I got back there with prisoners, I'd just miss them. Plus I wanted to personally interrogate them. I also knew we had a helo pad at the firebase.

"Hey, bro, I think I'll miss y'all by like fifteen minutes if I tried to get to BAF. Can y'all just come get me here?"

"We can't do it, brother, sorry."

"Okay, love you, bro. Gimme a shout when y'all get back from chasing wood smugglers."

Johnny grabbed the phone, "Hey, Sheff, get me some of those good Afghan Kush seeds from those booger eaters you're with. I know you've got some. My ol' lady wants to grow some sticky Kush out back of our house."

I laughed and then reminded him we were on a phone.

"Love you, bro! OUT!"

We went back out to the same area and rolled up every shithead involved. I turned them all over to the Afghans. I'm positive they got what was coming to them.

When we got back to base, I grounded my shit and poured a tall Jack Daniels on ice and turned on Platoon. We had some downtime, it looked like, so I slumped down on the nasty brown couch in the corner. Damned thing had apparently never been cleaned or moved. Eastern European jizz all over it. I swilled my drink down like a man and closed my eyes. "I'll be dipped in shit, New Meats, y'all gonna love the Nam, man, fo fuckin' eva."

I could hear a phone ringing. I opened my eyes and checked my watch.

Holy shit, I'd been asleep for two hours!

Then one of the guys from the other room comes running in.

"Hey, are you Sheff?"

"Yep, that's me," I answered.

"There's a Sonny on the phone for you," the guy told me.

My heart skipped a beat. It didn't make sense. Sonny should be on an op right now. I was confused for a minute while getting up off the couch, and my heart started racing. I knew something was wrong. I could feel it in my guts.

There was the red phone laying there on the table, off the hook. I'm thinking it's probably Noah. He's always in the mix. He probably got wounded and is on a MEDIVAC to BAF. I'd meet him and bring him some Jack, I thought.

I picked up the phone.

"Hello? Sonny?"

"Hey, man, it's Shane. He's dead, brother. Johnny got hit, too, bro… he's still alive, but he's passing. They're on their way to BAF."

"Johnny's still alive, right?"

"I think so, but probably not gonna make it, man. It's bad."

I had collapsed on the floor. I didn't mean to. Shit, man, what do you say? Marco came in and checked on me and I told him to get the truck ready. We'd be heading to BAF shortly. I grabbed my kit, go bag, Bible, cigarettes, and filled up the flask that I finished before getting to BAF.

We went straight to the hospital. There was Noah, blood all over his pants and shirt from carrying Shane.

"Hey, bro, where's Johnny?"

"They cracked his chest, bro. His heart was in pieces. He's dead, man. They both are."

I hugged Noah. We were all crushed.

"What happened, bro?"

"They both went out full hero. We made entry, and Shane exposed himself to kill a guy pinning us down. He got hit under the plate. He was down quick, bro. And Johnny, we all thought it was target secure and Johnny goes back into the room and there's a dude in a spider hole in the wall behind the door. He shoots Johnny in the chest above the plate. Then Johnny ripped the door off and killed the guy that shot him. Then he walked out and was pissed. "Well, I'm hit, I guess. I'm going back to BAF!"

I went over to the mortuary where the bodies were. As I entered the room, I saw the bodies laid out there. On the far side of the room, on two tables, they laid there. They didn't look dead to me, just asleep. I so wanted them to wake up. I pulled out my front and back plates from my kit. Each was wrapped with a flag. I took the American flag off my back plate and laid it over Johnny, and took my Bones flag off my front plate and laid it on Shane.

The mortuary staff came in. "I'm sorry for your loss. I'm sorry to ask you, but could you please identify the bodies for us?"

I stared down at Shane's face and his pathetic excuse for a beard and wiped my tears away

"This is Shane."

Then I looked over at Johnny. "And this is Johnny."

At the tarmac in BAF, we pulled the coffins out of the back of the combat hearse. I called cadence as we marched, carrying the coffins up through the ranks of hundreds of soldiers in formation. We set them down and secured them to the deck of an empty C-17. Me, Noah and Adams would be going back with the bodies.

Sonny came over to tell us goodbye.

"I don't know what to say," he said. "I feel like I failed them."

He was shattered and could barely get the words out.

"Love you guys. Send them off proper. I know you will."

And just like that we were airborne back to the states. I laid down next to Noah, in between the caskets rattling through the turbulence.

"Here, bro, here you go."

I handed Noah the flask and then thumbed my Bible trying to find some strength and comfort. I found it quick. Psalms 91 always comforted me:

> *"He shall give His angels charge over thee, to keep thee in all thy ways.*
>
> *They shall bear thee up in their hands, lest thou dash thy foot against a stone.*
>
> *Thou shalt tread upon lion and the cobra...*
>
> *The young lion and the adder shalt thou trample under foot."*

We buried Shane in Arlington, next to the others we'd lost from Blue Team already. Then we buried Johnny in Virginia Beach. After we laid our brothers in the ground, the reality of the situation was really setting in. I had to leave again and get back over. I didn't even make it home before pulling over and puking on the side of the road. It was time to get myself together.

I knew I had a brief time at home before heading back over to Afghanistan. That night, me and Leslie just laid there. I rubbed her belly and talked to the little guy, hoping he could hear my voice.

"Hey, it's Daddy." I looked and saw the love in her eyes as she gazed at me. "You think he hears me?"

"Of course, he does. Did you find out when you have to go back yet?" she asked.

"Yeah, tomorrow night. I know, it sucks. We still got three more months of deployment left. Anything can happen."

It was good to see Leslie, but very stressful at the same time. We had to plan the funerals of our best friends while trying to help out families and kids and all kinds of stuff going on. We got judged for everything. Families maybe didn't feel like we did enough for their loved ones or put up enough of a memorial or something.

My mind quickly switched to going back overseas to war. And so I did. We ended up killing close to four hundred Taliban fighters on that deployment and conducted a successful cross-border op into Pakistan, just to prove we could get to the Al-Qaida fighters hanging out in the FATA, the Federally Administered Tribal Areas. I shot a lot of guys but, that particular op, I got my one and only female kill. Blew this bitch's head off. She was total Haj, rolling in with a line of dudes toward my guys. They didn't see me and the other sniper worth a shit. We took the whole line of seven, crisscrossing our shooting from the flanks inward. They basically ran into each other and we smoke-checked every one of them. They'd flop around and I'd get another face-shot in.

When we got back home, a group of us were in really good climbing shape from the workouts and operating in Afghanistan, so we put a team together and climbed Mt. McKinley in Alaska, in memory of Shane, Johnny, and all the other guys we lost. It was a total kick in the balls but it meant a lot to me. Our whole team summited. For the record, Delta Force had a team on the mountain at the same time and none summited.

I came home from Alaska in time to take Leslie to Portsmouth Naval Hospital for a scheduled aversion. Landon still had over a month before his due date and the little guy was still head up. As the doctors tried to turn him, I saw his little heart beat slowing to almost nothing. The doctors started moving very quickly. The cord had wrapped around his neck. He threw me some scrubs and said, "Get those on. We gotta get him right now!"

I was terrified. I don't think I had ever been that scared. I thought I was about to lose him. I prayed over and over to the Lord to save him. "Lord, please deliver and protect Leslie and our child. Please God, in Jesus's name, I pray."

Then I heard a little hoarse cough and we caught our breath. He made it. The docs motioned me over there when they were comfortable with him breathing. Then, with shaking hands, I cut the cord on a tiny human that could fit in my hand. For the next four hours, I peered through the glass of the little incubator. Leslie was recovering so I had some alone time with him. It was beautiful and peaceful. I held onto the moment. After Landon was born, I really just wanted to stay there and be with him all the time.

I started thinking differently about going to back to war, but I knew I was far from done with that part of my life. We were still at war and I was good at it. The days flew by and once again I was saying goodbye to my wife.

I can't imagine a way not to believe in something supernatural because it starts to not make sense after a while, combat. It's like, how can we still be going? We're killing people and these things flash through your head and you just deal with them but, for me, the way I stayed motivated and continued on was because of my faith.

I've asked for protection. I've asked God to send His angels to protect us. Straight up, out loud, send me angels, protect our group. I know God doesn't need me to direct Him. But I've asked for these things. My experience with it all showed me the truth. Looking back, war was too easy for me. The aftermath isn't easy. Even finding sometimes, if I looked back on it, such a massive evolution of effort to be in the right place at the right time.

Like intuition. I was in combat and I was killing and men were being killed. We were testing ourselves against this other group of fighters, going out day after day, night after night and doing this to the point I was living for it. I couldn't wait for the next OP. I mean, if I'm honest, we all wanted to test ourselves in real combat.

We've been called everything—savages, sociopaths, serial killers, whatever. In a way, it's all a little bit true. What we are not is the guy who is gonna hand out a soccer ball to the kids and make sure everyone's got medical attention in the village and shit like that. We were the guys who were gonna go and kill people, period. In fact, we killed more bad guys during OEF and OIF than all the other groups combined.

The next three years ended up being some of the bloodiest combat any of us had ever been in. By 2011, our little Team was personally responsible for more than a hundred thousand high value enemy combatants killed and even more captured. Unfortunately, it came at an extreme cost of many heroes.

Chapter 12
NUMBER ONE MISSION

"INCOMING, INCOMING, INCOMING!"

We woke up in FOB Shank Afghanistan to loud speakers and sirens. It was the middle of the day in 2011. Guys were all racked out. Getting mortared was our daily alarm. We rolled into the briefing tent and sat down on what looked like church pews. The new CO stood at the front of the room saying something about new ROEs. He began to tell us there was a presidential directive to take the Afghans out on target with us. As if that wasn't enough, we were ordered to train them, also. It was so outrageously bizarre to have SEAL Team Six training a bunch of unvetted non-soldiers. It put all of our lives at risk for the sake of political aspirations.

"Okay, now, I know this is gonna come as a shock, but we've been directed to train and equip these Afghans so they can someday do these types of missions. You need to put your gear next to theirs and start eating together. Make them feel part of the Team."

It was very difficult to take this dip-shit seriously. I couldn't believe he kept a straight face or that he actually had a trident, or had a penis, or had balls. Let me put this into context. They took SEAL Team Six, the most elite surgical assault force in all of history, and made us bring untrained, unvetted, non-operating Afghani soldiers onto missions that were one hundred percent combat, one hundred percent of the time. Now we had to watch our backs from our "own" and babysit. The president directed this shit. This was some real brilliance. We actually caught guys on our target list that had joined the ranks to infiltrate.

I would just lay up on the rooftop with my sniper rifle and draw a bead on the Afghans while my guys were forced to train them. And then they would complain that we didn't treat them right. Guys were calling home and getting lawyers because we started having to do shooter statements. They thought we were too aggressive, and we thought they should definitely eat shit. My only saving grace was when I got a phone call from my buddies out in JBAD.

"Hey, bro, pray for us tonight… We're going in after number one!"

We all poured a tall drink, knowing we weren't doing anything that night, and headed into the JOC. We gathered around the comm ticker. This was a computer screen that updated all the radio communications, so we could keep track of what point of the operation the Team was on. We were kept in the dark as to the plan, like everyone else. I just knew my buddies were signed up for a one-way mission and I'd be praying for their protection until I heard otherwise.

When we saw GERONIMO come over the ticker we could barely believe it. The guys had just killed Osama. As happy as we were, no one celebrated. No one said a word until the ticker updated once again and we knew that all our guys made it out alive.

Oddly though, that operation made everything really weird for us at the command. We were all treated like we'd done something wrong because of the attention. It didn't help when the news media told the world that Seal Team Six killed Osama bin Laden. They basically painted a big red target on everyone at the command and created a lot of jealousy and envy within the ranks of special operations. It almost destroyed the command. There were reporters following guys when they left work. They hounded us anywhere we tried to hang out, exposed the places we frequented, camped out outside the gate to the command. They even hounded Joey Nobody, trying to find someone to give them inside information about the guys, who they were. You know, typical shit.

It was a short-lived high, though. The guys from Gold had switched out with us, and literally a week into their deployment, we lost a whole troop of guys when their Chinook was shot down coming in to help the Rangers out. The emotional toll on the command was unbearable. It seemed like a dark cloud had settled over the whole command, and it stayed that way for a long time. We were worn thin from trying to support all the families and all the funerals, and still manage our training and deployment cycles. Everyone was working to make sure every hero was treated with upmost respect. Despite being harshly judged again, I saw exceptional behavior from command members coming together. No one cared about bin Laden anymore. We just missed all our friends.

And then…this happened.

We were out in Arizona skydiving and clearing our heads. We had packed up and finished for the day and guys were already cracking beers. We had been tasked to do the new O2 mask testing for the entire military. So we entered into what I called HAHO Hell Week. My Team would do four HAHOs a day. We'd start out every morning with a jump around 3 a.m. We would jump from thirty thousand feet, and then the next one would be twenty thousand, and so on. We had to make sure the new masks could take all the punishment of the harsh environments we worked in.

I stared at the rows of packed parachutes off to the side on the beautifully cut packing green. It looked like a big green field and it was the area we used to pack parachutes. We wanted a nice comfortable calm area to pack because nobody wanted to screw up packing a parachute.

I sat down with my buddies, who were talking about some chick they saw jumping and our phones started blowing up. It was command recall. They sent us all home. There was some story about an American female who'd been taken hostage. I couldn't believe my ears.

Oh, hell, yes! I thought…

We flew home and drove straight from the airport to the command. We all gathered up in the Team Room around my computer. The FBI had sent us the proof-of life calls. I hit play and turned the speaker up. It was a woman's voice, wrought with emotion.

Panicked and terrified, she pleaded while crying, "I think I'm gonna die out here. I'm really scared I'm gonna die. Please… Please someone help me… Please, I'm sick, I can't get through this. I'm scared. Please help me…"

It was hard to listen to. But we did, over and over again. We all had wives, moms, some guys had daughters. I will say, there is something different that happens inside us when women and children are in danger. All I could think was that those who do evil and wicked things, especially to women and children, probably will someday have to deal with guys like us. I hoped it would be us.

We looked at the massive screen on the wall in the front of the Team Room. The ISR feed was from a Predator Drone. I could see a little camp area and there was a blonde chick under a tree. Also, a little farther away, out in the open, appeared to be a white guy getting pushed around the camp and slapped around a bit. There were two hostages: a guy and a girl.

Sonny was a master chief now, the highest enlisted rank in the Navy, as far as MOB VI goes, the highest ranking operator. Regardless of what officers may want to think, enlisted operators still run *that* command. Sonny went up to the front of the room to brief us. On the other massive LCD screen was a picture of the two hostages. I studied their faces for about five seconds and then realized they'd be the only two white people in the whole country that weren't where they were supposed to be.

"Hey, fellas, welcome back. These two were kidnapped by Islamic militants while working some kind of missionary aid or relief or whatever. Who gives a shit… They're hostages. Here's their location. Recce has the plan. It will most likely be a HAHO profile. Sheff, you good to go?"

I knew I'd be leading the jump in. "Yep, good to go!" I said.

"Okay, so they're both being held together. Washington wants us to go. Hostage rescue. This is what we do."

This was the kind of mission we all dreamed of. I was the Sniper Team leader and lead jumper. It was a good place to be if you're not a vagina. We went to our planning areas off the main room and pored over imagery, weather, historics, intel, everything we could get our hands on.

Then in walks Gold Dust. He'd taken a two-year hiatus to Monterey, California to learn Russian. I knew he was coming back to take troop chief and be the new 2-2. Most of us that were still around had close to a thousand missions at this point. We were tight.

"Gold Dust! Damn it's good to have you back, brother!"

"Well, I heard you guys had a hostage you needed help rescuing. Don't get all scared; Daddy's here."

I gave him a big bro hug… "Troop chief, huh? First Op out of the gates and you get a hostage rescue. Don't stress, though, bro, I'm gonna make you look like a rock star."

Medlow poked his head in. "Well, look at this precious reunion…

Hey, what are you faggots talking about? That hostage is kinda hot, right?"

We all laughed.

Gold Dust chuckled and said, "All right, let's get serious."

We immediately got to work putting this thing together. This was going to take everything we had learned from all our experience.

The next few weeks were spent impatiently waiting on word to go or not. They'd been out there about seventy days so far. We were getting pissed nothing was happening. In any case, we continued to train day and night. We'd set up every different scenario we could possibly come up with and continued to push ourselves harder and harder. We even got female role players to train with, hidden in the kill house with active shooters, and we'd do house runs all night long. Then range time. Then back to the drop zone. We had to live and breathe the kind of training at this level.

Hostage rescue was completely different mentally. It had to be. It was all about keeping the other person alive at all costs. As soon as the shooting kicked off, you only had seconds before someone put a bullet in the hostage, which meant no self-preservation. You'd disregard all the usual safety measures and tactics you would normally use on the battlefield. You absolutely must be ready to die for that person.

The time came and we gave our final briefs to the Sec Def and he approved the Op. They'd been out there about ninety days. I went home to spend one more evening. We'd be rolling out at midnight, heading to Africa.

I sat down at my desk and opened my Bible. *Because he loves Me, says the Lord, I will rescue him. I will protect him. For he knows My name. He will call upon Me and I will answer him...* I closed the Bible.

I walked into Landon's room. He was asleep. Leslie was pregnant again, due any day, another son on the way. I hoped I'd see the little guy. I looked back at Landon, and he looked so peaceful lying there. Innocent. I had to take it in for a minute.

Then Leslie walked in and sat down next to me. She was crying. She was a bit scared. Leslie knew what was about to go down. Landon woke up.

"Daddy, why is Mommy crying? Why are you crying?"

I picked him up out of his bed.

"I'm not, Bubba, we're okay. Daddy has to go away tonight."

He crawled up into my lap, "Daddy, do you have to go fight bad guys again?"

"Yes, little man, I do. There is a girl and she is in trouble and she needs Daddy and his friends to go and save her. I love you very much, Bubba."

"Daddy, I don't want you to go." He leaned in and hugged me.

"Don't cry, little man. I'll be okay. God has His mighty hand on us. He's chosen us to go and I'm going with the best guys in the world."

He sat up. "What will you do?"

I grabbed some of his G.I. Joes and a toy airplane and acted the whole thing out for him on the floor.

"We're gonna get on a plane and fly over to where the bad guys are. Then me and my friends are gonna jump out with parachutes on at nighttime, far enough away that the bad guys won't hear us. Then we're gonna sneak in like ninjas, and kill the bad guys and save the girl!"

He was smiling. He loved when I acted things out with G.I. Joes.

"Are you gonna get all the bad guys?"

"Every one of them!" I told him.

"Daddy, is the girl like Mommy?"

I looked at Leslie. "Yeah, Buddy, she's just like Mommy, but she's in trouble and she needs help right now. You've gotta be a big boy and take care of Mommy while I'm gone. Little brother is almost here. Okay?"

"I love you, Daddy," he said.

"I love you, too, little man."

I hugged his little body up on my shoulder and could feel tears going through my cammie top. I kissed him and smelled him. I just wanted to remember his smell.

Leslie came over and hugged us, and I said, "I got the CACO sheet done and our life insurance is square; everything's good, Babe."

She was crying and said, "I don't want to talk about that right now."

I hugged her and kissed her and told her I loved her. "Pray for us. We need prayer, Babe."

"Of course I will, nonstop."

My brother was out front at the truck. He drove me to the C-17 that was loaded and waiting on our private airstrip.

"Wish I was going with you, man," he said.

"I wish you were too, bro."

"I know you guys will crush it, man."

I said, "Thanks, bro, just pray for us, okay? I know you will. And hey, if something happens…you know what to do, bro. Make sure my boys get my Harleys and teach 'em what I would."

He put his hand on my shoulder. "I got you, man. I'll be watching from the Team Room. It's all good. God's got you."

He pulled the truck through the series of coded gates and drove out to the flight line, all the way to the back of the bird. We both got out and hugged.

"Love you, bro, see you after!" he said.

"Love you, too, bro," I told him. "I'll call you after."

We both smiled and flipped each other off. Then I boarded the plane.

Two in-flight refuels and we touched down in Djibouti, Africa about twenty hours after we had taken off. It was basically like Bagram Airfield, just in Africa. So just think everything was the same, except just a little shittier, as if that was possible.

The place was controlled chaos. There was equipment being staged and gear being prepped. Aircraft were being moved around the flight line. Ships off the coast of Somalia were being re-tasked to support us. It was a full-scale Navy recruiting commercial. The total operation cost was already well over a hundred million. That's what we'd spend to get one citizen back if possible.

Once we unloaded, I headed over to the JOC. It was crawling with a bunch of ass clowns who wanted to be a part but weren't. We had our sniper shack off to the left side of the wall of screens. I headed in to finalize the plan with my Team.

Next was a full Rehearsal of Concept (ROC) drill, where all players briefed their portion of the op. We were on Video Teleconference (VTC) blasting back to JSOC, the Pentagon, and the White House.

We were all standing around giant maps on the floor. Each department head briefed—first weather, then intel, then pilots, then key planners. I remember when the weather guy got up and briefed.

"Hey, guys, just of note, before I get into the weather and the high winds, there's gonna be a solar flare tonight. It's supposed to happen around the time you guys will be in the air and it might affect your communications and GPSs."

And then he started into the weather report and Gold Dust was like, "Whoa, whoa, whoa, dude, back up for a second…what did you just say? What solar flare?" he asked.

"Oh, it's kinda like a thousand nuclear warheads going off on the sun."

I forget how he described it, but we're like, "So our comms and GPSs are going to be messed up; is that what you're saying?"

And he was terrified. Poor guy got put on the spot in front of everyone. He was like, "Um, yeah, it could happen."

And we were all bitching among ourselves, "Are you kidding me, man, are we gonna roll twenty-four for that?"

"We're going no matter what," Gold Dust said calmly.

Then he finished, Intel briefed, and the different pilots all got up there. They moved little model helos and planes around and went through contingencies should there be a loss of aircraft or catastrophic failure en route.

"They all land here. The birds will land this order," one pilot explained.

The air traffic guys basically built out the dirt airstrip and schedule of all the aircraft so it was clear to all players.

Finally, after everybody had briefed their piece, the assault force briefed "actions on." Our brief was easy. My ground force commander gave a real quick snapshot.

"We're gonna jump out, we will land, we will walk, we will commence hostage rescue, we will return to base with the two hostages. Any questions for us?"

No one said shit. People were looking at us in disbelief, like we were some kind of aliens. Everyone knew we were the main effort. Really, the point of it all was blah, blah, blah, get us where we need to be and we'll take it from there.

Our personal "actions on" were briefed with my Team in another room.

We knew we'd be landing to the south because of the winds and walking north. As we approached the target area, we'd take a right and head in from west to east due to wind direction. We always wanted to come into the enemy downwind if possible. We didn't want the wind at our backs blowing our scent into their camp.

I usually wouldn't ever shower before ops, or even use deodorant that day. These dirt bags never smelled deodorant in their life and some dumbass lathering on the Old Spice could blow the whole op. Guys knew better than that, but why risk it, know what I mean? Or some new guy decides to take a dip of something other than Copenhagen. Mint Skoal, for example, and that could be the difference. In the past, I actually had to remove Iraqi and Afghan partner force soldiers from ops because some of those idiots would spray on cologne before we left the base. No deodorant by the way, just cologne. I mean those clowns just smelled like a bag of onions, Aqua Velva, and a sopping wet, three-day-old baby diaper. Anyway, where were we…

On this particular night, the bad guys actually planned to move the female hostage again. She had been out there probably in that spot for maybe thirty days and they had planned to move her this night but they didn't. They ended up staying put because they ate some lamb and had tummy aches, we found out later. Thank God. Muslims have a lot of problems with lamb.

After the OPORD, we all filed out. I grabbed the pilots who were over getting coffee.

"What's up, fellas? Welcome to DJ. I'm Sheff; callsign Fox-1. I'll be lead jumper and jump master tonight. You'll have me up on comms in the bird. Glad to have you with us tonight. Heard you boys came straight over from BAF?"

"All good, brother, nine-hour flight, but we're good to go. Just tell us what you need from us," was his reply.

I ushered them over to our private planning space away from the madness. Me and the other jump masters started in on explaining exactly what we needed.

We knew we'd need to pre-breathe under ten thousand feet for at least an hour to saturate our bodies with O2. I got to "actions on."

"So, for the jump tonight, I'd like to get the ramp open at three minutes out with a steady red. I want a green at thirty seconds out and flashing green red, green red for the release point. Guys will be under night vision and I want the lights flashing for a drop. Sound good?"

"You got it, Sheff. Flashing green red at the release point."

Everyone was still out doing final checks and Gold Dust called for all the guys to come into our room before getting jocked up.

I walked up to the front of the ready room and looked at my troop. "All, right guys, here's the deal. Tonight is different. Once the shooting starts, it doesn't stop until it's over. This is Hostage Rescue. We will accept rounds for these hostages. Stay in your lanes and watch your shots. Also, it sounds like we got some pretty high winds, so keep it tight on the jump. If you get lost, or there's a parachute malfunction, we'll get to you tomorrow. Clear? Gold Dust, you got anything?"

"Yeah, I do, you new guys, congratulations on finishing Green Team and getting to Blue. Hostage rescue for your first op. You boys hit the lottery. Come get your Bones patches, boys. Can't have you jumping in naked."

The three new SEALs and one new EOD guy stepped forward and Gold Dust put their patches on their right shoulders. We all went up and shook their hands.

"All right, assholes, let's not go sucking each other's dicks just yet!"

"Hey, fellas," I said, "y'all bring it in real quick. I want to say a prayer. Bow your heads."

Everyone got on a knee around me and put their hands on each other.

"Dear Heavenly Father, we love You and thank You for all You have given us. We ask on this night, Lord, for the special blessing of Your guidance and protection. Please surround us with Your angels. Please, Lord, let us not grow faint or weary. Please deliver our enemies under our guns, Lord, and deliver the hostages safely into our arms.

"Let Your will be done, and let us be used as instruments of Your salvation. Almighty God, it is in Your Son Jesus' name we pray and ask these things. Amen."

Chapter 13
ALL EAGLES OSCAR

Two flatbed trucks pulled up outside the high bay door and we piled all the parachutes on them.

I called out over the hustle, "Hey, jock up with a buddy. Two JMPIs before getting on the bird. Cypress is Zero Down."

The C-130 fired up and all four props were turning, blowing hot diesel air directly in our faces as we approached the ramp. I stopped short of the ramp to count everyone else on before boarding. Then I went up and down the line of guys sitting shoulder to shoulder. I had to check all their O2 bottles and make sure they were breathing off the plane's O2 and not their own bail-out bottles. We had a three-hour flight and would be jumping from twenty thousand feet. We'd need all the O2 in our bottles.

I finally sat down against the ramp in the darkness as the plane took off. We were airborne. My feet wouldn't be on land again until Somalia. I pulled out my little Bible and used my chemlite to illuminate Psalm 91.

> *"Because he has sent his love upon me, therefore I will deliver him. I will set him on high because he hath known My name..."*

We sat for about two-and-a-half hours. Most guys were asleep. I couldn't sleep. I hadn't eaten anything, either. I was wide awake, wondering how it would all go.

I stood up and got everyone's attention keying my radio.

"2-Troop, Fox-1. 20 minutes, 20 minutes to drop…Ground winds…30 knots gusting to 40."

I could see the reaction to my wind call on everyone's faces. We knew the winds were double what would have normally cancelled the jump. But this was no ordinary night jump. We accepted the risk.

"10 minutes, 10 minutes."

Guys were starting to stretch it out a bit.

"3 minutes, 3 minutes…RAMP!"

The ramp opened and I could hear a female voice in my earpiece. It was Draco 9-1.

"Fox-1, this is Draco 9-1, radio check, OVER."

"Draco 9-1, Fox-1, got you, Lima Charlie. We are one minute to drop over."

I stared out into the black abyss. There was no horizon, no lights, just an empty void.

"One minute!"

I turned to look at my Team one more time, glowing green through my NVGs. Each of those men would stare death in the face before the night was over, and yet each was willing to make the ultimate sacrifice, unafraid. I asked God to protect us.

"30 seconds, guys!"

"30 seconds! 30 seconds! 30 seconds!"

There was no more practice, no more training, no more make-believe. This was it, the moment of truth. I turned to look at the go-light, glowing green and steady. A moment later, it flashed red and green and I hollered, "Let's roll!"

Then I was diving into the abyss.

"One thousand, two thousand…"

I was already falling at 120 miles an hour, upside down, with my body slightly arched and with one hundred fifty pounds of gear strapped to me.

"Three thousand, four thousand, look thousand, pull thousand!"

My spring-loaded main pilot chute shot open, billowing to life in the frigid air. With a jerk, I was upright, falling fast, swinging wildly from side to side, then the canopy was fully open and the lines sang and twanged, and I found myself in a controlled descent.

I reached up with my gloved hands and released the steering toggles. Pulling right, I drifted right; left and I went left. I looked down at my GPS—I was traveling at a ground speed of 109 miles an hour and radioed the guys to warn them.

"2-Troop, Fox-1. Passing through 17,000 feet on a 1-8-0 degree bearing, with a glide ratio of 10 to 1. Guys, we are cooking at 109 miles per hour."

At the lower altitudes, the winds were still howling.

"Passing through 10,000," I said, "Saddle turn to the left and stop on 1-6-0 bearing, then square up and let 'em fly."

That ride under canopy seemed like forever, floating in space with moments of vertigo wondering if I was still descending. We couldn't see the ground anywhere. I couldn't make out one single light or even the horizon, which I thought was very unusual. All I could see was a faint red hue from the tiny compass light on our tac-boards on our chests and the grainy dark green glow of our night vision, almost rendering them useless due to the lack of ambient light. I still couldn't see the DZ, and it looked like we were heading into a dust storm, so I radioed the support aircraft for help to see the ground.

"Draco 9-1, Fox-1 can you send a sparkle in a figure eight on the DZ, please? We are having some trouble finding it."

Immediately, I looked out and saw what looked like an infinity sign being painted on the top of a dust storm below us. At 5,000 feet, I was still hauling ass. I was now facing into the wind and moving backward.

"Hey, guys, everybody turn into the wind at 0-9-0. I don't care where you are in the stack, turn into the wind."

We were still falling through the blackness, not a hint of land in any direction, not even a glimmer of light anywhere. I had never before seen a night this dark.

A few minutes later, I got back on the radio, "Okay, boys, we're passing through 4,000. Hold station."

We were still flying backward, and still going way too fast, so I braced myself for a hard landing. I hit the ground and ass-ended my way into a thorn bush, which hurt enough to make me love being alive.

I then turned to watch the other guys land, one at a time, and several of them got dragged across the desert by that bitch of a wind. Through my NVGs, I could see them tumbling across the desert floor, struggling to cut themselves free of their canopies.

One guy radioed in to say he had landed about four football fields away—not bad, given the circumstances—and he began hiking his way back.

Then we could hear screaming. I thought one of my men was hurt and barked into the radio, "Whoever that is, shut the hell up and we will come help you!"

But he didn't shut up because it wasn't one of our men; it was the hyenas. I took a look through my thermals and saw them out there in the brush, dozens of them, studying us, their eyes glowing and ghostly.

"Not tonight, fellas. We have a job to do," I muttered under my breath.

We got busy changing. Every man found another to link up with and hold security, while his buddy changed out of his jump gear. I ditched the jacket and the thick gloves. It had been blistering cold on the way down, but on the ground it was more than one hundred degrees in the middle of the night. Why would anyone want to live in this place? I thought. I was back down to my t-shirt and kit.

I reached into my ruck for my sniper rifle, gently reassembled it, then I snapped both locking pins into place. I screwed the suppressor into position, listening to each muffled click. I inserted a magazine, sent the bolt home, and was ready to go. I could see a tree in the near-distance. I put my laser on the trunk and married it to the crosshairs in my scope. My rifle was properly sighted. Then I quickly screwed a suppressor onto my pistol and made sure there was a round in the chamber, laser-checked it, too, then stowed it in my holster. I was ready for assault.

The guys and I moved toward each other and stuffed our parachutes and extra gear into parachute bags in one central pile. The last guy showed up without his chute, covered in dirt and looking like he'd been on the losing end of a fight.

"Believe this shit?" he asked. "I got dragged for three hundred yards. My main chute is going to make a tent for a very happy dirt farmer."

When all the gear was in a pile, we rigged it to blow. We would do that right after the mission ended, when we were on our way out.

Our Air Force combat controller radioed the pilot, thanking her for lighting up the DZ. Then we radioed the guys in the Blackhawks—they had to inflight refuel three times to get to Somalia—to let them know we were about to move out.

"2-2, this is Fox-1. Recce is up and ready."

"Roger, Delta up and ready."

"Echo up and ready."

"Roger that, 2-Troop. This is 2-2. Recce, take it out."

We had planned an hour from boots off the ramp to Recce stepping off in patrol. We made it in fifty-nine minutes.

"2-Troop, this is Fox-1…passing checkpoint 4."

I knew in my heart God was watching us. And a whole bunch of other folks were watching also. I knew that every aircraft, both manned and unmanned, was streaming live feed to JSOC, the Command, the Pentagon and the Situation Room at the White House. Knowing we were being watched only added to the stress. On the plus side, however, other more capable eyes were watching the surrounding terrain for potentially unpleasant surprises, and it was good to know they had our backs. I also knew my brother was watching with his Team and praying for us.

At Checkpoint 2, we turned east and, after another kilometer, we began circling toward the target area. When we were seven hundred meters from the target, not yet within view, we radioed for an update, but the clouds had moved in, blotting their view, and a solar flare was messing with the radios.

"I guess we're on our own, thank God," I said under my breath as I looked up at the sky.

As I watched the clouds completely blot out the stars, I was internally grateful. We kept moving and stopped again at five hundred meters. This was our ORP, the last bit of cover before we committed irreversibly to the assault. That was the beginning of one of the longest hours of my life. The night was so black, our night vision was grainy and looked like the black-and-white noise on an old TV set, shaded with a dark green hue.

As we left ORP, I passed one final, "Snipers are moving," over the radio and off we went. The wind was in our faces at a solid twenty to thirty miles per hour. This is exactly what we'd planned for so as to hide our sound and smell.

I took a look through my thermal scope, "Holy shit."

I keyed my radio, whispering, "All stop."

I couldn't believe what I was seeing as I studied the contrast of white and black in my thermal scope. I keyed again.

"Bad news, boys, everyone's awake."

My stomach sank into my shoes, and the void was immediately replaced with a belly full of adrenaline that started its course once again. I could feel the veins in my neck begin to pulsate.

I whispered, "Moving," in conjunction with a hand signal and began to move forward as if I was entering an ice-cold bath. My senses were so heightened I could hear the inhalation of my breath and the wind blowing through the scrub brush.

I called to my snipers to move to the flanks, then I gave the signal to the troop lined up behind me. As I put my arms straight over my head toward the sky and put my hands together, the troop began to break apart in two elements. I was the center and had a team of assaulters on each side of me, with snipers on each outer flank. This produced a wedge formation.

The pace was on me now and everyone maintained his spacing of about six feet. I felt as though I was in a cannon whose wick was lit and raging and any moment was going to ignite the powder.

We continued painfully slow, pausing after each delicate step. I would step softly, then slowly shift my weight off my rear leg and repeat as my eyes had become immovable from the dead space that lay ahead. I studied the darkness for any sign of movement. It was so dark that my mind began to make up images. I whispered to my number three, who was the far right flank, and asked for a distance update.

He replied, "Two hundred meters out," and then started calling out every ten meters to give us a countdown because we still couldn't see the target area.

He called one seventy meters out and I started to make out large trees and what appeared to be vehicles. I raised my rifle up and looked through my thermal scope, still moving forward, and immediately picked up two heat sources. I whispered, "All stop, all stop" and everyone once again froze on my mark.

Two armed sentries were on watch under a tree. Both stood up and were looking in our direction. They were maybe fifty yards from us. One yelled out in Somali.

I passed, "Moving. Let's go, guys."

I felt the adrenaline now in full circulation as my step hardened its purpose. The guys on either side of me continued in perfect unison, looking briefly left and right to keep spacing as they charged forward. The two guards started to get excited as we slowly closed the distance, and they began yelling more.

I immediately aimed with my rifle and put my laser sight on the face of the one yelling. My laser was instantly met with ten other lasers from my Team. Both of these bastards' faces glowed, like a green sun, completely covered with our sights. These two animals began running away from us and into the camp behind them.

Keying my radio, I passed, "Pick up the pace," and we began to slowly jog. The guys maintained spacing and stayed in their lanes.

As the camp became clearer through our night vision, I saw the two guards that had just made it back to the rest of the fighters, and we watched all nine of them scramble to get on line using the micro-terrain for fighting positions.

We maintained our pace, and I was now close enough and it was quiet enough to hear the sounds of the belt-fed machine guns and AKs being racked. Now it was only a matter of seconds before the night sky turned day.

We continued to advance the pace and were pretty much at a full run at this point, trying to close the distance and get a visual on where the hostages were. So far as my eyes sprinted left and right processing the images coming through my night vision, my brain was only building pictures of heavily armed Somalis with beards and man jammies on.

It took everything in us to hold our fire as we watched the enemy maneuver to fighting positions in what was seemingly a slow-motion dream. I watched as the enemy fighters took their best aim at us. I felt as though I was floating in total slow motion, studying the vision in front of me, begging my eyes to find the hostages. The first explosion of my eardrums crackled as the belt-fed machine guns kicked off first. The AK fire followed. My left-flank snipers accepted the challenge of two fighters who were squeezing the triggers of their PKMs, sending hundred-round belts of 7.62 bullets through the night, like millions of little red shooting stars zipping through our ranks.

Both fighters were defaced and de-souled as my snipers searched for the next life to end. The night was a full-on eruption of chaotic horror. We continued forward, trading blows with the enemy.

My troop chief yelled from behind me to watch our shots. Make sure they count. I swung my rifle over and dumped four rounds into another machine gunner. The first two hit the top of his chest and left arm as he lay prone on his PKM, causing him to drop his head onto the top of the rifle. I followed up two more rounds into the top of his head, exploding his skull apart.

I continued to engage the enemy with my Team, surgically taking each shot. I felt every sensation of recoil as I pulled the trigger and still worried because I didn't know where the female hostage was.

I could feel the heat of the barrel, smell the gunpowder, and taste the oil from the chamber, still lubricated from when I sprayed down my gun before leaving the base. I felt the first stage of my trigger gently click as I squeezed, telling myself to slow my breathing and steady my trigger squeeze.

You must make this shot, I thought. Did I kill? Is she okay? Where is she?

We were still moving forward at a slow jog and then I saw two of these demons standing five yards apart wielding AKs and engaging our line.

Little did I know she was on her back right in between the two dirty little bastards. My teammate to my right and I engaged both these pirates, crisscrossing from their heads to their chests, dumping two shots into each available mass. We continued to fill them with bullets, ripping their insides apart as their dying bodies collapsed and their souls were being torn out to meet their buddies in hell. And, over the gunfire, lo and behold, as I saw between the convulsing, dying bodies, her face appeared like a horrified child from under a blanket.

We were in full flight at this point and I dove, throwing my gun to the ground so as not to burn her skin with the barrel. I was merely a body shield at this point, anyway. My teammate and I dove on top of her, holding her head by our armor and covering her with our bodies.

Another teammate straddled us with his legs, standing over the top of us, offering yet one more layer of protection, waiting earnestly to serve it up.

I keyed my radio, "Jackpot Hotel, Jackpot Hotel, Hotel is Oscar."

As we laid on her, we told her, "Calm down; we are Americans. Calm down, we are here to save you. Are you shot or hurt in any way? We need to know. Are you able to walk?"

She said, "I have no shoes."

"No problem. I'll carry you," I replied.

I picked my head up and looked around to see if we could move yet.

"When the shooting dies down, I'm gonna pick you up and we will run for a while."

She looked at me and said okay in a shaky, unsure voice.

"You ready? Let's go." I picked her up and yelled, "Let's go, boys."

I carried her cradled in my arms, shielding her and holding her head down with my hand. The boys grabbed my rifle and made a human shield around us as I sprinted out with every bit of energy I had left. I ran back the direction we'd come from, knowing we had more friendlies back that way. I ran until my body collapsed and I could run no more. I stayed on top of her with her head under my chest and her body protected by my own.

The two PJs made their way to us and began taking vitals. I looked at her and said, "You're safe."

She asked, "What if more come? More could come."

I simply said, "We are SEAL Team Six. We will kill anyone who tries to harm you now."

I think me saying that actually seemed to calm her down a little bit. She asked me if there was any way to get her shoes. I replied by getting up and running back to the mat she had been lying on and finding her sandals. Upon my return, it was as if she was upset to ask me about a personal bag she wanted to take with her. It was a small black bag that had her notes and personal items in it. I returned running to the mat, thinking to myself, I'm getting everything that's laying here this time. When I got back, I had a suitcase and her bedroll and asked if she wanted to keep any of it.

She answered, "No, just the little black pouch."

Our Team continued to search through the carnage looking for any good intelligence. They dragged the weapons, bullets and rockets into an area designated area by EOD to clear all and prepare for blowing in place. There were five belt-fed machine guns, multiple RPGs, multiple AKs, and a shit load of ammo. It was impressive for nine Somalis. The other hostage had been recovered and was also carried to my position.

One of the new guys had jumped on him during the firefight and ran him to us once the enemy were all dispatched.

I told the hostage he should thank God he was captured with an American.

He replied, "Thank you," and then looked at her and said, "I told you they would come, I told you they would come."

I offered them both some water and my Copenhagen to him.

Then she asked me, "Have you talked to my husband? Does my family know?"

"I haven't personally talked to them, but I do know they are waiting for you to come home. In a few moments, a helicopter is going to come and land. You will get on and you both will fly to another place not too far from here. There you will get on a plane that will fly you to where your family is waiting for you. You are safe now. No one will harm you again.

"My name is Justin, and it was the pleasure of my life to come and rescue you from this hell. I will probably never see either of you again, but please know that we will continue to pray for you and your recovery. For now, it is time to go home."

She squeezed our hands tightly, saying, "Thank you."

Then I told her, "If you really want to thank us, don't ever come here again."

As the Blackhawks came in and flared, I took her left arm and another teammate got on her right. My number two was running in front, putting his flashlight onto the ground behind him as we ran to help her not step on all the thorny bushes we were running through. We got them to the helo and placed them on board. My teammates and I took a knee and waved to the pilots. They gave us a thumbs-up and disappeared in the brown-out.

As I was watching the helos disappear into the darkness, my ground force commander passed over the radio back to command, "0-1, this is 2-1, I pass nine EKIA, two Hotels Oscar, BREAK, All Eagles Oscar!"

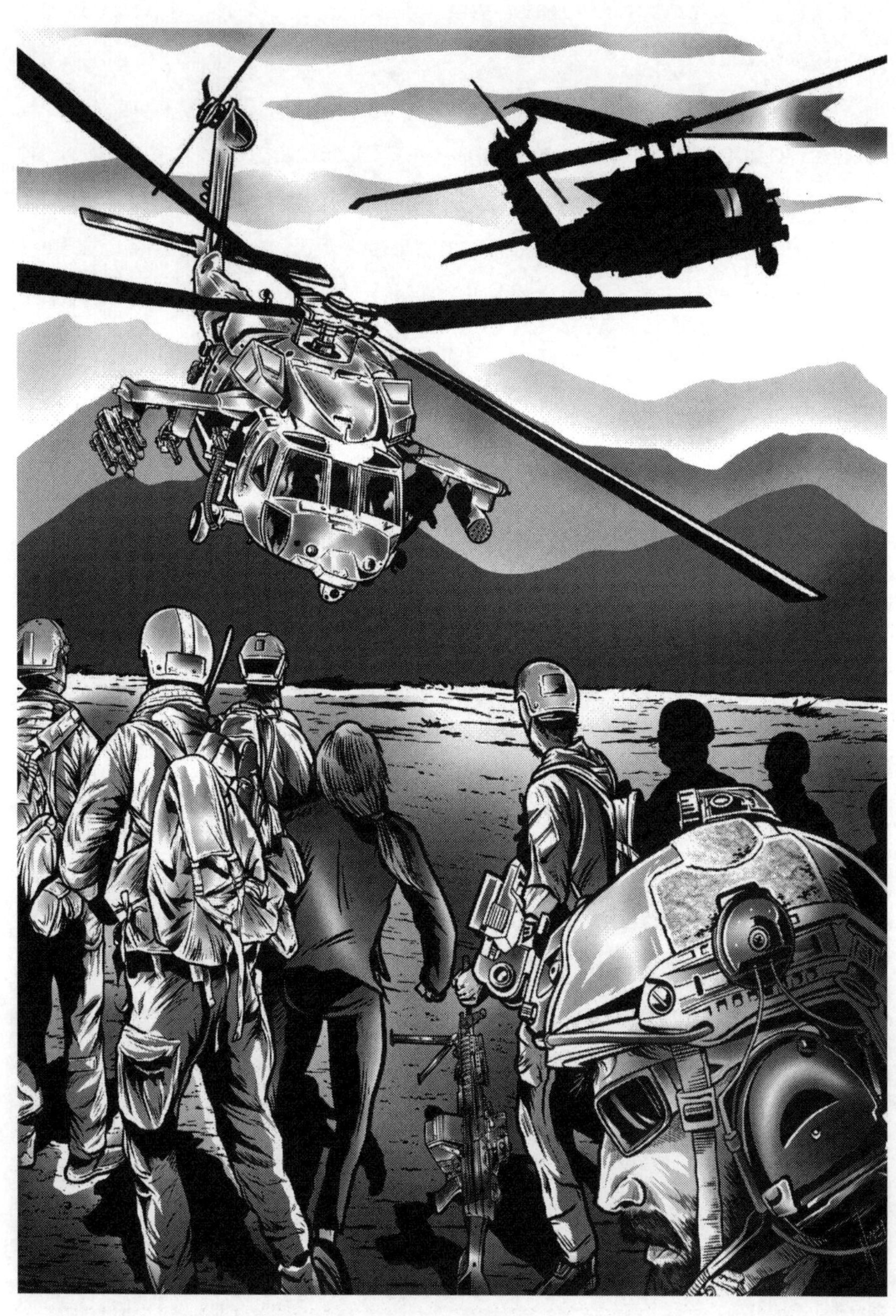

Chapter 14

THIS IS THE END

After we'd rescued the hostages, the rules of engagement for regular deployments had gotten so messed up that none of us wanted to operate under the new terms anymore.

We were tasked with a new mission to train, advise and assist an Afghani partner force to try to do what we do. And we had to live in the same compound as these guys. We were ordered to.

Look, our attitude toward it all was that there may probably be some good decent guys in the bunch. But we had no business with any of them. We were there to kill bad guys and rescue people. That's it. None of us had signed up for this horse shit. They put us all at grave unnecessary risk. Repeatedly. All I cared about was the guys. Those cunt leaders put us in harm's way so they could show how great their men were doing out there. It was for recognition. They were made to look good by guys like me. That's why they hate us.

I couldn't wait to see my family. I knew I'd never be going back overseas again. It was a good feeling. My head wasn't right for it anymore and that was hard to swallow. I ended up becoming an instructor down in training and really enjoyed it. It was the first time I was out of a Team and on my own. I was training everything from up-and-coming operators to teaching support personnel how to wear night vision and shoot a gun. Then shit went downhill quick.

Looking back, I should have taken a break somewhere in there. I didn't want to take a break because we were still at war. I guess I just thought, This is gonna die down someday soon. I know that I'm good at this. I need to keep going. I felt obligated to the Team not to leave. This is why a lot of the guys…every one of these deployments, we'd see the psych afterward and I was always like, "No, everything's good, family's fine, good to go," because if I said anything other than that I could be off the Team.

But my time was done. I was a stranger in my own home.

Sunday morning, Landon was sitting at the bottom of the stairs. I was trying to tie his shoes. I was trying to just be his dad for a minute. It was hard to concentrate. Colton was on the floor crawling around playing. We were supposed to be going to church. I was losing my mind. Nothing was making sense. I was slipping. I knew there was something wrong. My body and mind were smoked. I secretly started seeing the command shrink.

I walked in and sat down on the couch in his office. "What's up, Sheff? What can I help you with?"

I unloaded everything I thought about the command and home life.

My back was so jacked up I could hardly wear plates anymore. Turned out I needed disk replacement surgery as well.

"I can't even focus enough to read a text message…much less an email. What the hell is wrong with me?"

He asked, "About how many breaches do you think you've done?"

He had his notepad out.

"Hundreds of blasts. I've been knocked unconscious four times, completely out."

"Okay, Sheff, no worries. You probably have one or more TBIs. What about PTSD?"

I said, "That shit doesn't exist, Doc. Isn't there some pill you can give me that makes this all better?"

He looked at me. I was getting emotional already.

"Hey, man, don't worry, okay, Sheff? Let's see what we can do. I'm gonna talk to the command surgeon if that's okay with you and we'll come up with something. I've got some heavier meds that will get you sleeping better. That seems to be a huge problem for a lot of you. How about nightmares?"

"Every night. And night sweats. I'm done operating. I need to get fixed."

A few days later, a box of pills showed up, at least ten different prescription medications that I can remember. Eventually, they stepped my meds up to the brink of what was legal. One was for nightmares, but it would also lower my blood pressure, so I had to take another pill on top of that for the blood pressure stuff. Add to that Ambien and oxy for pain and wash it down with the occasional stiff drink.

It didn't matter anymore. Hell, nothing seemed to. I didn't feel anything. I didn't laugh or cry or have any emotion anymore. For me, for a little bit, that was just fine. It was actually a bit of a relief. I'd just lie on the floor in a daze and watch my kids play. I could have gotten shot and I wouldn't have cared.

At dinnertime, I'd kiss my kids on the head and go out and eat in the garage, if I ate at all. I'd sit out there and want to be inside but I couldn't do it. I couldn't sit at my own table. I looked at my family and I felt defeated and completely out of place. I wanted to be with them more than anything, but I couldn't even have a conversation with them.

After I went away to Bethesda to run some tests, I was diagnosed with severe PTSD and multiple mild TBIs. I also had two ruptured discs that would require full replacement and fusion. I got medically retired. Leslie came up to Maryland to pick me up. On the way home, Leslie drove and I just stared out the window.

"Babe, I'm sorry," she said. "I know that's not exactly what you wanted. But we'll get through this together. I'm with you no matter what."

She always supported me.

"Honestly," I started, "I think it's a relief at this point. I'm done."

I got home that night and went upstairs and just stared at my boys sleeping.

And, just like that, I was out of the Navy. No ceremony, no farewell. They just took my command badge and escorted me out like I'd never been there. I figured things would get better now. But that's when it all took a turn for the worst.

Almost nightly, I'd sleep on towels and wake up screaming into a pillow. Stuff that grown men don't do. It was a black hole. I saw my Bible on my nightstand and just stared at it. I wanted to read it so bad, but I wasn't about to open it. I didn't feel worthy to. I'd fallen away from God, it seemed. It was to the point where I wasn't leaving my room much anymore.

I started drinking heavily. My depression worsened. I figured that Leslie and the boys would get my million-dollar life insurance policy, even if I killed myself. I couldn't wait. Just had to have the right moment.

One morning, after a particularly bad nightmare, I decided I'd had enough. Watching Leslie from the window, I could see her down in the driveway loading Colton in the car. She was taking Landon to school. I could see him down there playing while she buckled in his baby brother. They looked happy. She was always there for me, too. No matter how messed up I got, she just loved and prayed for me.

I entered the closet and sat down cross-legged. I thought they had left for school and, honestly, I don't know why I thought it okay to blow my brains out in the closet. I wasn't figuring much, I guess. I put the gun to my temple and…

"Daddy, Daddy, why are you crying?"

Landon opened the door. I shoved the gun under my leg and wiped the tears away with the back of my hand. "I'm okay, Bubba. Where's Mommy? I thought y'all were gone."

He looked up at me and hugged me. "I just wanted to tell you bye, Daddy. We worry about you."

Leslie entered the room with baby Colton, looking for Landon, and quickly surveyed the scene. Landon looked up at her. She was staring at the pistol grip sticking out from under my leg.

"Babe, no! What are you doing? We have to get help right now." She sat down next to me and started praying.

In truth, I wanted her to challenge me, to tell me to just go ahead and do it if that's the way I felt. Then I could be free to just pull the trigger. But she never did. I wiped the tears away and looked back at the Bible. I had gone in with one intention and the Lord had given me another.

It was still very hard to keep a thought, or have a conversation. It was mush in my head; I'd get extremely depressed, extremely mad at myself. I couldn't even get a sentence or a thought out because I would lose myself somewhere in the thought. Soon after finding myself on my knees in the closet, though, I was able to find help. There was a new cutting edge treatment for the brain and it wasn't medication. It was magnetic resonance therapy and it worked. They used a magnet to force a specific frequency on my brain, over time, and "asked" the neurons in the injured parts of my brain to start firing in sequence again. It's just a little bit at a time, eight seconds on the minute for thirty minutes a day. I was willing to try anything. I'd go in everyday for a half hour.

They'd re-scan my brain every five treatments. They could actually see traumatic brain injuries. They could see what side of my head the blast was on. It wasn't talk therapy. It was like, "We see that you have PTSD, and we're gonna adjust the affected areas."

A month into it, I wasn't taking hardly any medication anymore and I was actually sleeping again. Two months into it, I actually saw a difference in myself. I could rack and stack thoughts in my head. I could focus again. Four months later, I was off almost all meds and actually sleeping through the night. I even got off the oxy and used cannabis for pain instead.

The real truth of it is, we are all going to die and that God saved me and can save you and will save you. And, whatever anyone may believe or not, for all the pills and therapy and treatments that might've had a role to play, what really saved me was Christ.

It was late as I sat in my office trying to finish what I was reading and both my boys came in and got in my lap. I had a newfound sobriety in my eyes. The Bible was open to Psalm 91.

I finished out loud to them, *"He shall call upon Me and I will answer him. I will be with him in trouble. I will deliver him and honor him; with long life I will satisfy him and show him My salvation."* I closed the Bible.

"Daddy, what does the Gospel mean?"

"It means Good News, Dude. It's a good message. The Bible tells us that God so loved the world that He *gave* His Son."

He butted in, "You mean Jesus?"

"That's right, Buddy. Jesus lived a perfect sinless life, and did miracles and wonders and was crucified by the Jews for claiming to be the Only begotten Son of the Living God. God allowed this execution of Jesus to happen in order to atone for all of sin of all mankind. Our Savior died in our place. And they beat Him and whipped Him and spilled His blood. Then they nailed Him to a cross, big enough to support the weight of a man. Yet He opened not His mouth. Then, after receiving vinegar on his bleeding lips from a sponge, he said, "Tetelestai!" And bowed His head and gave up the Ghost.

"This is good news because the Bible says that the wages of sin, what we earned from God for our sin, is death. And the punishment is everlasting torment in a lake that burns with fire and brimstone."

"We're all sinners, right, Dad?"

"Yes, Baby, we are all sinners. No one is exempt. That's why Jesus had to die and atone for all the sins of all of the world. None of us would make it on our own. We aren't good enough. But God loves us. He made us in His image. We are all very special to Him. That's why Jesus took on flesh and dwelt among us.

"God hates sin but He loves you. God wants you to be saved. This is why He gave His Son Jesus and why Jesus is the Christ. We need a savior. He said, 'I came to seek and to save that which was lost.'"

Colton spoke up, "But He's still alive, right, Dad?"

"Yes, He is because God raised Him up three days later and He walked right out of the tomb. And all His disciples and family saw Him. And then hundreds of people, at one time, saw Jesus ascend up into Heaven where He sits on His throne at the right hand of the Father. And whoever believes in Him is saved and goes to heaven to be with Him forever someday when they die. We will see loved ones and even people we've read about in the Bible will be there like Moses, and Aaron, and even King David. Even Mary from Bethany, the sister of Lazarus, will be there, who anointed Jesus' head and feet with precious ointment in preparation for His burial."

Landon looked at me. "Jesus is there right now, right, Dad?"

I looked down at my boys and said, "Reach over with one hand and pinch your arm..."

They both grabbed some skin on their arms and looked at me.

I said, "Jesus Christ is as real as you and me are this very instant and all the ones to follow! From everlasting to everlasting, He is God. And, if youconfess with your mouth the Lord Jesus, believe in your heart that God raised Him from the dead, you will be saved and He will raise you up on that last day. For by grace are you saved through faith, and that not of yourselves; it is the *gift* of God, not of works, lest any man should boast."

I looked at my two boys. "Do you believe what I have told you and shown you?"

"Yes, Dad," they said together.

"Can I help you pray and tell God that you believe?"

"Yes, Dad."

"Bow your heads and let's pray together."

They bowed their heads.

"Dear God, I know I'm a sinner, and I'm sorry for my sins, I believe that you, Jesus Christ, died on a cross for my sins. I believe that You rose from the dead three days later and You are alive right now and forever. Please save me right now, Lord Jesus. Thank you for saving me. Amen."

We immediately went to the bathroom and filled up the tub. I baptized both my boys as my little brothers in Christ, in the name of the Father, the Son and the Holy Spirit. Leslie stood beside the tub while I squeezed Colton's nose with my left hand and, cupping his head with my right, I gently leaned him back and said, "I baptize you, my little brother in Christ, in the Name of the Father, the Son, and the Holy Ghost, buried in the likeness of His death," and gently lowered him back under the water and lifted him back up out of the water… "Raised in the likeness of His resurrection."

Landon was next…

I hugged my boys and told them that Baptism is not what saves but God's grace through faith alone, in Christ Jesus alone, and that water Baptism is an act of obedience to God.

"Now go get in bed and I'll be there in a second to read to you about when Jesus returns."

"Okay, Dad, we love you," Landon said.

"I love you both very much, too."

I sat down between my boys on the bed and opened my Bible up to Matthew.

> *"And, as he sat upon the Mount of Olives, the disciples came unto him privately, saying, Tell us, when shall these things be? And what shall be the sign of thy coming, and of the end of the world?*
>
> *"And Jesus answered and said unto them, Take heed that no man deceive you. For many shall come in my name, saying I am Christ, and shall deceive many. And ye shall hear of wars and rumors of wars: see that ye be not troubled: for all these things must come to pass, but the end is not yet. For nation shall rise against nation and kingdom against kingdom: and there shall be famines and pestilences, and earthquakes in divers places. All these are the beginnings of sorrows. Then they shall deliver you up to be afflicted, and shall kill you: and ye shall be hated of all nations for my name's sake.*
>
> *"And then shall many be offended, and shall betray one another and shall hate one another. And many false prophets shall rise, and shall deceive many. And because iniquity shall abound, the love of many shall wax cold. But he that shall endure unto the end, the same shall be saved. And this gospel of the kingdom shall be preached in all the world for a witness unto all nations; and then shall the end come.*
>
> *"When ye, therefore, shall see the abomination of desolation, spoken of by Daniel the prophet, stand in the holy place, Then*

let them which be in Judaea flee into the mountains: Let him which is on the housetop not come down to take anything out of his house: Neither let him which is in the field return back to take his clothes. And woe to them that are with child, and to them that give suck in those days!

"For then shall be great tribulation, such as was not since the beginning of the world to this time, no, nor ever shall be. And except those days should be shortened, there should no flesh be saved: but for the elect's sake, those days shall be shortened.

"Then, if any man shall say unto you, Lo, here is Christ, or there; believe it not. For there shall arise false Christs, and false prophets, and they shall show great signs and wonders; insomuch that, if it were possible, they shall deceive the very elect.

"Behold, I have told you before. Wherefore, if they shall say unto you, Behold, he is in the desert; go not forth: behold, he is the secret chambers; believe it not.

"For as lightning cometh out of the east, and shineth even unto the west; so shall also the coming of the Son of man be. For wheresoever the carcass is, there will the eagles be gathered together.

"Immediately after the tribulation of those days shall the sun be darkened and the moon shall not give her light, and the stars shall fall from heaven, and the powers of the heavens shall be shaken:

"And there shall appear the sign of the Son of man in heaven: and then shall all the tribes of the earth mourn, and they shall see the Son of man coming in the clouds of heaven with power and great glory.

"And he shall send his angels with a great sound of a trumpet, and they shall gather together his elect from the four winds, from one end of Heaven to the other.

"Now learn a parable of the fig tree; when his branch is yet tender, and putteth forth leaves, ye know that summer is nigh: So likewise ye, when ye shall see all these things, know that it is near, even at the doors. Verily I say unto you, This generation shall not pass, until all these things be fulfilled. Heaven and earth shall pass away, but My words shall not pass away.

"But of that day or hour knoweth no man, no, not the angels of heaven, but my Father only. But as the days of Noah were, so shall also the coming of the Son of man be. For as in the days that were before the flood they were eating and drinking, marrying and giving in marriage, until the day that Noah entered the ark, and knew not until the flood came and took them all away so shall also the coming of the Son of man be.

"Watch therefore: for ye know not what hour your Lord doth come. Therefore, be ye also ready: for in such an hour as ye think not the Son of man cometh."

I flipped over to Revelation VI.

"AND I beheld when he had opened the Sixth Seal, and, lo, there was a great earthquake; and the sun became black as sackcloth of hair, and the moon became as blood; and the stars of Heaven fell unto the earth, even as a fig tree casteth her untimely figs, when she is shaken of a mighty wind.

"And the heavens departed as a scroll when it is rolled together, and every mountain and island were moved out of their places. And the kings of the earth, and the great men, and the rich men, and the chief captains, and the mighty men, and every bondman, and every free man, hid themselves in the dens and in the rocks of the mountains; and said to the mounts and rocks, Fall on us, and hide us from the face of Him that sitteth on the throne, and from the wrath of the Lamb: For the great day of His wrath is come; and who shall be able to stand?"

I flipped forward to 19:11.

"And I saw heaven opened, and behold a white horse; and He that sat upon him was called Faithful and True, and in righteousness He doth judge and make war. His eyes were as a flame of fire, and on His head were many crowns; and He had a name written that no man knew, but He Himself.

"And He was clothed with a vesture dipped in blood: and His name is called The Word of God...

"And out of His mouth goeth a sharp sword, that with it He should smite the nations: and He shall rule them with a rod of iron: and He treadeth the winepress of the fierceness and wrath of Almighty God. And He hath on His vesture and on His thigh, a name written, KING OF KINGS, AND LORD OF LORDS."

I flipped forward to 22:12.

"And behold, I come quickly; and My reward is with Me, to give every man according as his work shall be. I am Alpha and Omega, the beginning and the end, the first and the last. I am the root and the offspring of David, and the bright and morning star. He which testifieth of these things saith, Surely I come quickly.' Amen. Even so, come, Lord Jesus."

ABOUT THE AUTHOR

SENIOR CHIEF SHEFFIELD is a recipient of the Silver Star, six Bronze Stars with Valor, a Purple Heart, and a host of other medals and commendations.

He now serves as president of All Eagles Oscar Foundation.

The callsign "All Eagles Oscar" refers to the callout we hope for following combat operations. It means all of us Americans, "Eagles," are okay and headed back to base. But it refers only to the visible injuries sustained on the battlefield. Often, it is the invisible injuries that change our warriors' lives. It's a burden carried by their families as well as those brave men and women who serve us.

The specific purpose of All Eagles Oscar is the distribution of funds, by the foundation, to help provide physical and mental relief to our veterans, active duty service members, and their families suffering from the many combat-related afflictions. In furtherance of this purpose, our goal is to help fund the most progressive, innovative, and EVIDENCE-BASED treatments available.

Our primary purpose at AEO is to recognize these veterans and get them the treatments that are having major results so they can continue to serve their families, communities, and nation in new and positive ways.

One of our primary focuses is raising funds in order to treat combat veterans suffering from Post-Traumatic Stress Disorder, Traumatic Brain Injury, Persistent Post-Concussion Syndrome, dependency, addiction, and chronic pain management. We will continually seek cutting-edge treatment modalities and therapies that will restore function and purpose to lives that have been altered following injuries and stresses received in combat. We've had a tremendous success with combat veterans truly getting better, thanks to the treatments we support and our many awesome donors.

Neuro-modulation: MeRT is a pioneering technology that uses Magnetic e-Resonance Therapy aimed at restoring optimal brain function. Advanced imagery is able to identify areas of the brain that are not functioning properly, and MeRT treats problematic areas with the goal of restoring optimal neurologic function using safe, non-invasive, non-pharmaceutical neuro-modulation.

Integrated rehabilitation and performance: With the help of world-class performance centers, we aim to narrow the gap between pain, injury recovery, and optimal performance. Recognizing that restoration of daily function is a critical part of recovery for a wounded veteran, we also realize that returning our veterans back to an *optimal* state of physical health has a significant benefit, not only to physical health and pain relief, but also emotional and psychological well-being.

New Programs: We will continue to seek out the latest cutting-edge, effective treatments, and therapies that will help restore the lives of combat veterans and their families. We are dedicated to aggressively seeking out avenues to ensure the cost of treatment will not inhibit the ability of our nation's warriors to receive the care, treatments, and recovery they have earned defending our freedom.

We need your help! More military deaths occur from suicide than in combat. Military suicides are at the highest level, and make up 20%

of national suicides. More than three hundred thousand veterans have been diagnosed with PTSD from serving in Iraq and Afghanistan, and combat veterans have an alarming number of traumatic brain injuries that far exceed the statistics of any other segment of our population, including professional athletes.

JUSTIN K. SHEFFIELD

HELP CHANGE A HERO'S LIFE
MAKE AN IMPACT

All Eagles Oscar relies on the generous donations of people like you to ensure that we can make a difference in the lives of our combat veterans. There is no more worthy cause than to assist our nation's heroes in recovering from the physical and sometimes invisible injuries received defending our great nation and protecting the freedom we all so deeply cherish.

For more information on how to help, or to make a donation, please visit our website at alleaglesoscar.org

Made in the USA
Middletown, DE
17 May 2020

95411205R00106